THE *Power* OF KNOWING

K P WEAVER

Copyright © 2020 Karen Mc Dermott

First published in Australia in 2020
by Making Magic Happen Academy

www.makingmagichappenacademy.com
www.karenmcdermott.com.au

All rights reserved. No part of this book may be used or reproduced by any means, graphic, electronic, or mechanical, including photocopying, recording, taping or by any information storage retrieval system without the written permission of the copyright owner except in the case of brief quotations embodied in critical articles and reviews.

This is a work of fiction. Names, characters, businesses, places, events and incidents are either the products of the author's imagination or used in a fictitious manner. Any resemblance to actual persons, living or dead, or actual events is purely coincidental.
National Library of Australia Cataloguing-in-Publication data:
Mindful Magic/Making Magic Happen Academy
Romance – fiction

ISBN: (sc) 978-0-6488203-2-1
ISBN: (e) 978-0-6488839-5-1

A Knowing is not just a thinking matter, it is a feeling matter of fact that instigates a confident action.

KAREN MCDERMOTT

CONTENTS

INTRODUCTION — 7
The Knowing Strategy — 11
Knowing — How do you Prepare for it all? — 13

FEEL IT — 16
Knowing and Your Why — 23
Knowing and Your Relationship with Divine Energy — 28
Knowing and the Importance of Priorities — 34

THINK IT — 39
Knowing and Choice — 41
Knowing and Your Calling — 44
Making the Choice to be Your Own Success Story — 46

ACTION IT — 50
The Golden Rules of Knowing — 52
Knowing and Taking Action on Inspired Thoughts — 54
Knowing Yourself — Go Within or Go Without — 56

Knowing Musings — 60

Knowing in Embracing Adversity — 60
Knowing and Embracing Different Practices — 63
Knowing and the Essence of Faith — 68
Knowing to Heal. — 76
The Knowing in Writing — 78
A Group Knowing Conversation — 81

KNOWING STORIES — 89

Knowing with Joanne Fedler — 90
Knowing with Michelle Weitering — 101
Knowing with Karen Weaver — 109
Knowing with Bernadette O'Connor — 112
Knowing with Jane Talbot — 126
Knowing with Elizabeth Gilbert — 135

IN CONCLUSION — 149

*Three-step Knowing strategy –
Feel, Think, Achieve.*

KAREN McDERMOTT

INTRODUCTION

A Knowing is not only a thinking thing, it's so much more!

Many of us perceive a *Knowing* to be something we think but I know it is a whole lot more. When you truly learn how to *Know,* it will guide you through tough times and navigate you towards higher levels of success when setting intentions. You will never find yourself hopeless for there is always something to strive towards. It helps you appreciate and enjoy the journey as much as the destination because you surrender to endless possibilities. You will discover aligned opportunities around every corner waiting for you to embrace them. *Knowing* is a truly magical way to navigate life.

Are you ready to embrace the power in *Knowing*?

Knowing is a sacred skill, one of the universal gifts we all have within us but not all have the ability to access it.

Are you familiar with the concept of *Knowing*?

What if I told you that you already hold the key to something special that will change every aspect of your life — and that I can teach you how to use it? Would that make you sit up and listen?

For years I have trialled and tested my three-step principle and can confidently share my thoughts and experiences. I have researched my findings and found other successful people who have kindly shared their *Knowing* stories to help you understand the principle in more depth.

A *Knowing* may be perceived as a spiritual experience of a connection to a higher level and one without foresight, with only hope as a bargaining tool, but it is quite the contrary. Intuition is an important part of *Knowing* as it assists with the feeling of connection, but it is not the only element of *Knowing*, in fact it's a third of the process.

You already have the ability to know. We all have it within us. *Knowing* is something we can all learn to navigate, regardless of our religious beliefs or personal circumstances. Learning how to access your *Knowing* will be a life skill that will bring you to the highest heights. You will learn to make unwavering decisions without fear of failure because you will know the choices you have made are based on a *Knowing* strategy that works only to serve you and align with your higher good.

When navigated through intention, Knowing reaches a level of no limits. Anything can be!

When the philosophy of *Knowing* found me, I knew I was

gifted with the knowledge of something that has the power to shift the perspective of a large number of people. That when this new thought concept is embraced it will see people across the world reaching new levels of success in the key areas of Love, Life and Business or whatever they choose to put their mind to.

I have used the *Power of Knowing* for many years and if you have followed my journey you will see I have made major achievements. I have built a portfolio of successful publishing houses from the seedling of an idea because I channelled my *Knowing*. This allowed me to make decisions with confidence, overcome challenges and navigate my life towards multiple successes in a short time. I use my *Knowing* to navigate my life in many directions. In between the covers of this book you will learn how you can use yours.

Knowing is energising. When you feel confident in the choices you are making, no energy is being wasted on soul-draining thoughts.

In this book I will introduce you to what it is to live a life with no fear in the choices you will make, because there is no fear in *Knowing*. As well as discovering the three main principles of *Knowing* I will share with you numerous *Knowing* musings followed by some *Knowing* conversations and stories. I value the power in story to deliver wisdom and hope you enjoy the insights from the awesome people who share their *Knowing* stories and receive the gift that is woven through their words.

The heart of knowing is knowing what to ignore.

RUMI

THE KNOWING STRATEGY

So how does it work?

I use one strategy in manifesting everything in my life – the *Knowing* strategy. When I don't use this strategy I make mistakes and experience unnecessary and often costly detours when working towards achieving my dreams and goals. Destiny is there for us all to embrace but many of us settle with playing safe or get so distracted by the dazzling attraction of external objects that we waste time in reaching our highest potential.

It is when we reach our highest potential that the race for success ends and a new more relaxed pace of life is there for us to embrace if that is what we choose. There is profound comfort in the *Knowing* that you have succeeded in manifesting a deep-rooted desire, that all of your hard work and risk-taking has paid off. It is from this position that the world is your oyster and you can stand confident in the *Knowing* that you have made magic happen and can do it again if you so choose.

So, what is this *Knowing* strategy?

There are three simple steps.
1. Feel it.
2. Think it.
3. Achieve it.

Often a *Knowing* is understood to be an intuition. It isn't, although the channel of intuition plays an important role in *Knowing*. True *Knowing* takes intuition to the next level. Intuition is often perceived as a feminine quality and because it is channelled through the frequency of love it is often more easily accessed by women. However, *Knowing* is something we all have the key to unlock. Through this book you will discover how to access YOUR *Knowing*.

Understanding the power in a *Knowing* is a life skill. One that you will develop to become increasingly aware when a message is reaching you and instinctively act upon it with the three-step strategy that I will talk about numerous times throughout this book.

This is often from an external source. Keeping open and aware is imperative. Successfully receiving and processing messages is vital.

Knowing — How do you Prepare for it all?

If your life is already full then be mindful that things will have to shift to allow the new to enter. It is often good to do a life declutter when setting an intention. I do it all the time. I start to feel overwhelmed and constrained so I begin to shift my focus to clear the backlog and avoid filling that void with more work. In doing so I create the space required for the magic to happen.

If you have already read Book 1 in this series, *Mindful Magic*, you will understand the principle of true magic happening when you create the space to let it in. How can it shine into your life if your life is at capacity, bursting at the seams?

Clearing the way ensures you will be able to channel your *Knowing* effectively.

How to declutter:
1. Write a list of everything you have filling your life right now. EVERYTHING!
2. Prioritise your list into three categories: what you want to do, what you must see through now and what can go.
3. For the least important list start imagining what it would be like to clear those tasks from your schedule. Imagine the space it would make in your life.
4. Do not plan to fill that space, keep it open until the right opportunities come your way. Fill the extra time with soul- nourishing activities.
5. Repeat every six months.

WHAT I MUST DO	WHAT I CAN DELEGATE	WHAT CAN GO

Knowing yourself is the beginning of all wisdom.

ARISTOTLE

FEEL IT

You have probably heard how your feelings will help you generate the energy required to attract what you want. We have the power to control our feelings so we can manipulate our destiny and attract any number of desires. I have used this successfully on many occasions. So how is *Knowing* different?

Knowing is your internal compass, a skill you were born with and can access anytime. It's true power in the alignment with your true purpose and highest potential. It's the next level from *The Secret* by the wonderful Rhonda Byrne. It is having true ownership of who you were, are and choose to become. Watching *The Secret* kick-started my experience of being responsible for my thoughts.

Watching Louise Hay's *You Can Heal Your Life* gifted me permission to be loving and gentle and still make amazing things happen in my life through navigating my thoughts. It's all physics in the end and it is important to realise the impact your thoughts and feelings have on your world and the world around you. It is within your reach to influence those thoughts and feelings so you can live your best life and in doing so, do your bit to help others live theirs. It's all about choice.

Mastering the Law of Attraction can attract wonderful opportunities to you. I have become so in tune with this frequency that sometimes I am afraid to think because I instantly set in motion channelling whatever my heart desires.

This shouldn't be a problem but it can be, because it is my mind doing the desiring, not my soul. My soul is connected to my divinity, my true purpose, the purpose that makes my heart sing. My mind will not know what that is until it presents itself to me, therefore I can mindfully manifest something that is not truly aligned or destined for me. That is where *Knowing* comes into play.

The first step of *Knowing* is to Feel It. When an opportunity is presented to you, how do you feel? Do you want to grab it straight away and run with it? If the answer is *yes*, that is wonderful. It is so exciting when bright shiny new opportunities come into our lives. It is at this point when you can instinctively move to the next stage of the *Knowing* process, which is to Think It.

I am not suggesting you talk yourself out of the opportunity. This step is simply asking yourself, 'Is this aligned with my divine purpose?' If the answer is *no* then walk away, because it is a distraction that will waste your time on your journey to your highest potential. Your highest potential is the journey you want to be on as it is the most fun, least stressful and the destination is somewhere you will never want to leave.

If the answer is *yes*, then you move to the next step, Action It. This could be simply saying *yes* or it may be pursuing a lead, completing an application or following through on a thought.

In my experience, when I have an inspired thought, I feel I need to take action right in that moment. That is generally a get-straight-on-to-it *Knowing*. Magic can happen when you act on that.

In December 2015 Oprah came to Australia. I booked tickets for myself and my beautiful friend Donna. If I was going to experience Oprah, I wanted her to be with me. Luckily she said yes and we were really looking forward to it. A week before the event an idea came to me that as Oprah is a book lover, a gift basket of books would be a fabulous gift for her. I was oblivious to all of the celebrity gifting companies that charge thousands of $$$ for the privilege, but I knew there was a way and I just had to find it.

I posted on Facebook to ask if any of my contacts knew anyone who worked at Perth Arena where the event was to be held. I got a reply and gave them a call. They guided me to the event management company that was coordinating the tour. Even though it was at the most inconvenient time for me I knew I had to call in that moment. I got through to someone who gave me an email address for the person in charge of the gifts. They emailed back with instructions to have the basket at a certain reception at a specific time.

Interestingly, that was the morning I was hosting the playgroup Christmas party at our school so on the day I delivered the basket dressed up as Santa's helper. It all made great PR. A lot of my entrepreneur friends heard about what I had achieved and reached out to ask if they could have my contact, which I shared freely but none of them got a reply.

I know that time and circumstance aligned to make that happen. I felt the opportunity, thought on whether it aligned with what I wanted to achieve, and finally took action in the very moment I needed to and magic happened.

When you are channelling your *Knowing* things happen fast so you need to be ready to act and know that it is aligned with what you are aiming to achieve. This was a fun time and I often get asked if Oprah ever contacted me. No, she didn't but I know that when time and circumstance align again, I can mention the gift basket she received at her first Australian venue and it will assist with a more meaningful interaction.

A *Knowing* generally goes against all logic, it is quite often the last thing you think you should be doing at that time in your life. It calls you and you must listen. It's important to remember that every event, interaction and moment in our lives is working towards our highest potential. It's that simple. The problem these days is that we get so distracted on the journey because there are so many possibilities.

It's the choices we make at those integral times that determine how long we will take to reach our destination. It is wonderful to have the privilege of choice because so many people have had that taken away from them as victims of circumstance.

In 2006 I went through a tough time. I suffered PTSD (Post Traumatic Stress Disorder) after a life event shifted my very being. The feeling of 'things will never be the same again' was something that shocked me to my core. I loved my life and juggled so many things. I didn't realise that it is then that things can crumble. Looking back I can see I wasn't identifying the signals happening around me. I wasn't being mindful and this life event occurred to set a ball in motion so I would take action and move forward towards my highest potential.

I always knew I was destined for more than small town living. It frustrated me a little because I would have loved to have been content in my heart to be still and live a simpler, less complicated life. The reality was that for me, that would probably never be the case. Moments of quiet, yes, I treasure them, especially when I am recharging my batteries ready for the next adventure. But content with stillness forever? No, not me. It isn't in my DNA. So, during my year and a half of stillness I took the time to consider moving to Australia. This is not something I would ever have considered beforehand. My mother and I had been to see a tea leaf reader and when she said that I would live in Australia, I totally blocked it because I was so close to my family there was no way I was going to not see them every day.

But the events that had occurred created the possibility in my mind so I applied for our residency visas for Australia. It took me one full month to collect all the paperwork we needed. I had to be determined and focused but I did it and then left it in the hands of faith, knowing that if this was to be, it would be.

A year later we still hadn't heard any word and were living in limbo, not knowing what action to take. But actually, we were taking action by being there in that moment preparing for it all. Life was aligned even though it wasn't good. There were things we needed to endure and experience to get us aligned with the divine timing of what we were about to do. I never lost the *Knowing* that this was what we were supposed to be doing. I remained focused on the goal and got on with aligning myself with it, even though there was no certainty. All I had was faith that everything was happening and when I needed to take action, I would *Know*.

We got our visa call at the very moment I was picking up our wedding rings from the jewellers. When things align like that they are affirmations that you are on the right track. We planned to leave on September 1st, the first day of spring in Australia and autumn in Ireland. I was thirty-five weeks pregnant with my third child. It looked to be the craziest thing to be doing in my life at that point as we had just completed building a new house and were locking it up to pursue the unknown. Yet I did know this was the very thing I was supposed to be doing. I never wavered or questioned the process; I just *Knew*.

I share stories like this because we can all learn from each other's stories. It felt as though my life was falling apart but it was actually coming together. I was gifted the unwavering *Knowing* that what I was doing was totally aligned with my highest purpose, even though at the time I did not know what that higher purpose was. Make sense?

It does take courage to have this type of unwavering faith in *Knowing* as quite often it goes against conventional thoughts and practices. Your courage to connect directly with YOUR source of purpose will be rewarded and save you heaps of time in the pursuit of your goals if you roll with it and take immediate action when you reach step three in the *Knowing* strategy.

The only true wisdom is in knowing you know nothing.

SOCRATES

Knowing and Your Why

'Knowing your deep WHY stimulates your willpower for change'
Levi Newton

Many people grow up with restrictions. These restrictions are put in place by our parents, society and other sources and stem primarily from fear. This is fine but how are we supposed to learn to navigate our inbuilt protective system when we have been protected from using it for so long? This system is the Power of Knowing. *Knowing* when it is safe to act and *Knowing* that we are moving forward guided and protected from harm is a powerful internal instinct that so many people are not familiar with using due to external 'nannying'.

I know how it goes, I am guilty of this too. I am a mum of six and I feel it is my job to protect my little beings but I have become increasingly aware that it is more beneficial to them if I see my role from an alternative perspective. That is to guide them and part of that guidance is showing them how to connect with their *Knowing* because that life skill will protect them way beyond my gaze. *Knowing* when something is aligned and when it is the right time to take action is a gift to our little ones.

The ultimate goal for those who embrace *Knowing* is captured in that split-second moment where you have the unwavering ability to say yes or no.

Learning how to activate this tool and navigating it so it is always working aligned with your highest intention is a skill that can be developed.

Where do you get a Knowing? My dear friend, you already have it, we all do, but through the generations we have lost the natural ability needed to access it intuitively.

That is why this book is important and why we all need to learn how to *Know* again.

Personal power is something that is not treasured as it should be in this day and age. I am astounded that so many people are willing to hand over their power to others. Do you not realise that the power to make our own choices, walk our own path is worth so much more than any gold coin? We need to alter our perspective on what is valuable, where life's wealth truly resides. Believe me, you can have all the money in the world but that might come with huge burdens to bear.

Is it not ideal to walk our own path fulfilled because we *Know* we are aligned? The energy of feeling aligned is where life's magic happens. It is an undercurrent and you can see it in those who are truly aligned with their true purpose. They are comfortable in their own skin, glowing because they are living their best life for them; growing in spirit as well as in life.

We are human and it's normal to seek outwards for guidance, it is something we are conditioned to do. The problem with this is that when we do this, we also hand over our power, which is connected to the outcome of any given situation.

Think about babies. They cry out when they are in need of something but they don't give over their power; that remains their own. Yes, it is influenced by those who care for them but instinctively their goal is growth of mind, body and spirit and they do it well.

So why is power important?

This book is called The Power of Knowing because at the very core of *Knowing* is the realisation of the power we have to make unwavering choices in our lives. Choices that are fully aligned with where we are on our journey and our desired destination.

Opportunities present themselves daily. Many people struggle with making instant choices and they miss the real opportunities that have been snapped up by those who do have this ability.

It is about aligning yourself with your highest intention, an intention that is aligned with your soul purpose, so that when time and circumstance align for you, you are ready to say *yes*. This allows the flow of magic to happen.

Please know that aligning with your true WHY and then making it happen through a *Knowing* strategy is not selfish, in fact it is quite the contrary. Imagine a world where people answered their calling and pursued their purpose. Would that not be a divine world? Believe me, there will still be people who are happy to have uncomplicated jobs to make money because their priority is to live a simpler existence. That is fine. There will always be people who are starting out on the road to pursuing their purpose and so will do what is required to make that happen. But they will do it with gratitude, knowing it is a lever forward to activating their goal.

Once you pursue your purpose with loving intention then you will achieve it faster and even bring others along for the ride.

As Elizabeth Gilbert states in one of her posts whilst writing *Big Magic*, it is wonderful to pursue our passion once it doesn't harm someone else.

The benefits of living through your Why:
1. You live your life on purpose and aligned with the highest version of yourself.
2. You give your best to the world.
3. You will inspire others and show up as a leader in your realm.
4. When a 'why' is the essence of all intention, in there resides a power that is almighty.

Exercise: What is your Why?

*To Know is to move
forward in confidence.*

KAREN MCDERMOTT

Knowing and Your Relationship with Divine Energy

When writing this book, I endured a few blocks which hindered progress. I know when this happens in my books it is because something needs to be revealed. This doesn't help when your distributor is waiting for a delivery so with reluctance I put the book on hold and gave it the grace it needed to flow to me. *Knowing* is the second of my master gifts to live a life without fear and on purpose so I honoured the 'no fear' part and distracted myself with other projects until what needed to come to me did so.

Then one day I saw a post by one of my biz friends on Facebook about having a session with another of my biz friends, international psychic Rebecca Gibson. I am usually guided very confidently through my own *Knowing* and quite literally that is the reason for writing this book, but the call was loud and I *Knew* that Rebecca had something I needed to know. So I answered the call and booked a session. I imagine the energy between us was at very high levels because the internet was playing up. As we both live life on a high frequency that was to be expected. This was also our first face-to-face interaction — well, on Zoom.

We hit it off straight away and she asked me what questions I wanted to ask.

'What do I need to know?' I asked.

Watching this woman at work was wonderful. Rebecca spoke about my work and saw it exactly as it is and that I am very much at the core of it all. Then other questions began to flow and the final question came to me like a bolt of lightning so I asked about this book series.

'You need to connect with your relationship with God,' she said.

This caught me off guard but then it all became clear.

Knowing is all about having faith, living without fear. The penny dropped that our *Knowing* is at the essence of Godliness. We are the masters of what we achieve in life, we can make things happen and have so much more influence over our destiny than we even allow ourselves to comprehend. Sometimes this stems from conditioning and limiting beliefs that we are exposed to as we grew into who we are today. It is often easier to accept what we have been taught rather than challenge our own thoughts and have the courage to explore the internal calling wanting us to listen and navigate our personal path to our individual destiny. No two destinies will be the same because everyone walks a different path. We all have a different personality so even if the goal is the same, the formula for achieving it and the journey taken to reach that summit will be different. And as I always say, 'Everyone has a story to share because no two stories will be the same.'

The world has so many religions, all with a higher source that is honoured as a master of that religious orientation. It is always wonderful to have a positive loving leader who inspires masses of people to do beautiful things in the world but I can never get my head around any God inspiring people to come from a place of hate or revenge. This saddens me because I know these actions stem from fear and it is universally known that God does not live in fear. God lives in faith and hope and there is no fear associated with these actions. When you are filled with hope and are faithful that every step you take is aligned with your higher purpose, you will feel fulfilled and have no need to bring another person down. There really is enough for us all to share. Everyone has a different agenda and just because someone has something you want it doesn't mean there is any less for you.

If we morally eradicated greed and fear as a global motion and allowed everyone to be treated humanely; if we were all taught to deal with life's situations with loving intention, then conflict would not escalate to warfare. Harmony would ripple across the globe. One leader who embraces this type of leadership is New Zealand's Prime Minister, Jacinda Ardern. How she dealt with a terrorist attack was amazing. There was no fear in her response, only love and sadness. Sadness for the loss and empathy for the pain of fellow humans whose lives were changed forever at the hands of another fellow human. She didn't speak his name and allow him the media exposure he probably hoped for. The world saw only the loving actions of a prime minister who leads with her heart; who is trusted by her constituents and who makes other leaders take notice that there may be another way to lead rather than through force.

God is a three-letter word that holds so much power and has been interpreted in so many ways by different religions and that is fine so long as it doesn't hurt someone else. I know God is almighty, a power so much bigger than anything we could ever comprehend. Individually we are unique beings so there is 'no one size fits all' religion; we have to embrace an authentic, deep-rooted connection within ourselves. Connect with who we truly are and then bespoke our relationship with God, so that our connection is divine.

My spirituality is individual. It isn't governed by a set of rules and regulations. It is authentic and love filled. Anything I do for another person I do out of genuine choice, because I want to, not because I feel I should. Your connection with God should be free-willed, not forced upon you by society or because you fear the repercussions of what your family chose to follow.

I grew up Catholic. My beloved granny was a devout Catholic, the beautiful church was at the end of our park and most of our teachers were nuns, with some priests in the later years. I attended school in Ireland in the 1980s and religious studies was a big thing. There were statues all around the school just as in the church. They were sacred and every school was named after a saint. We were slapped if we did something wrong. I cannot imagine what I would do if a teacher slapped one of my children in this day and age!

I was pretty good and quiet so I never got slapped but I do have the mental scars of witnessing others being slapped with meter rulers, or a teacher's ring being thumped into a shoulder. This is nothing compared to what my mother had to endure in the 1960s. The nuns would make her scrub floors instead of learn because she was from a lower class family in the community, instead of helping their family out, which I am sure would be God's will. The nuns would abuse the system and judge my mother and many others because of their family status. I don't believe God would discriminate. My mother never really brought us to church or spoke too much about the emotional and physical abuse she endured at school. I know shame was one emotion she felt and she over-compensated with her children; we never went without.

I share this because taking the opportunity to understand your roots and re-establish your connection with God will allow you to connect at a deeper level with divine energy, therefore having a deeper connection with the highest version of yourself. Sometimes it is a story that can be rewritten. *Knowing* is so much more effective when you know through the channel of unconditional love.

Have as much faith in yourself as you would in your beliefs. For you are the essence and power that comes with making miracles happen. When you focus that energy inwards you will be a better person to share with the world. Many of the big players are the biggest believers in themselves and others follow their journey.

Knowing is not enough, we must apply.
Willing is not enough, we must do.

JOHANN WOLFGANG VAN GOETHE

Knowing and the Importance of Priorities

Do you know the importance of priorities? Do you know what your priorities are right now?

A conversation I heard from Elizabeth Gilbert in Perth helped me realise the importance of priorities in our lives. I have realised how important it is that we grow alongside our priorities and allow them in some sense to help us navigate our way through life. She said many people set intentions but they don't make them a priority. So how are they supposed to happen?

We can come up with all of the excuses under the sun for something not happening but I am going to call you out on it if you have not achieved an intention you have set. It is because you didn't prioritise it.

As for a lot of chapters in this book I will funnel my life experiences to the themes in discussion. Currently, we are going through the 2020 global pandemic and priorities have adjusted virtually overnight. My adjustment has not been too significant as I actually live every day connected to my home base. I do have an office and enjoy the division it gifts me between work and home life. However, setting up a makeshift office at home again isn't an issue for me because that's how I roll during school holidays anyway. It isn't ideal but I get on with it because being there for my kids when they are young is a priority for me, a choice.

I am not saying the global pandemic has forced people to succumb to unwanted priorities; in fact, I am saying the opposite. It has been a true gift to many to reset their priorities and be gifted the time for their mindset to adjust. Isolation may seem like torture for some and yet many people choose to isolate regularly without a pandemic because it gifts them time to go through the motions of adjustment.

I know when I am evolving or making a choice to change an element of my life, I set the intention and prioritise any adjustments that need to happen. When things are changing around you it can feel very unsettling as the cogs and wheels of your familiar life begin to adjust speed and fine tune to your new speed. That's okay and you will allow it to happen when you are aware of what's happening. But if you are not an aware person it can feel like your world is falling out from underneath you. In this case it can make a person resist or fear any outcome because faith is required during this process and there are no guarantees with faith!

Faith is the essence of *Knowing*. Have you ever watched someone who is going through something huge and thought, 'Wow, if that was me I would be all over the place?' Yet they are just going through the motions of it, confident of the outcome. That is *Knowing* in action. I can assure you that person does not know exactly what the outcome will be but they have faith in the process. They set a powerful intention for their goal to happen and prioritised it in their life. When they do this through their *Knowing* they understand the next step will present itself and they will know what action to prioritise to achieve the greatest outcome. Feel It, Think It, Action It!

> "It is not a daily increase, but a daily decrease.
> Hack away at the inessentials."
> *Bruce Lee*

When you start to build traction on your path your priorities become more important. I have had to adjust priorities along the way and find new ways of managing what I love best, which is to help stories find their way into the world. After reading *Do Less, Be More* by Susan Pearse I stopped spreading myself thin teaching the same thing over and again and instead thought outside the box. How could I serve more people more efficiently? It was then the Everything Publishing Academy was born. I put a lot of content and energy into the academy and had an amazing bunch of people in there. I did this for a couple of years and when it was flowing along nicely and not needing me so much, I chose to prioritise my personal passion for sharing my thoughts in this book series. I founded my Life Magic group and in 2020 we have been doing a gratitude challenge where every day I post a graphic and share what I am grateful for that day. It is a beautiful energy and many of the group share what they are grateful for each day too.

Have you visited your priorities recently?

Are your priorities your choice?

Many of us choose to be parents and gift a lot of our time to nurturing our children to adulthood. Yes, it's hard work but a choice and we prioritise that. Many of us choose to build a career or take on a job and make that a priority too and that is fine also. These are not sacrifices, they are choices and the hard work associated with them and all of our priorities are our choices. The priorities I would like you to revisit are those that are not your choice and no longer serve you.

> **'Things which matter most must never be at the mercy of things which matter least.'**
> *Johann Wolfgang von Goethe*

We need to regularly check in with what we prioritise in our life because as we grow we outgrow a lot. Just because you prioritised something last year or five years ago doesn't mean you have to keep it a priority for a lifetime. If you want to, then that's wonderful but if something is only a priority for a season of your life it is important that you set it free so it can find its way to someone else who will value it.

Personally, I feel too many people don't prioritise themselves and it leads to a lot of resentment and disconnection. Prioritising yourself is not selfish. It is vital for a harmonious society. When you meet your own needs it means you have the best of you to give to others. I truly believe this with all of my heart. If you want to live a life filled with life magic, which I hope you do because you are reading the Life Magic series, then I suggest you prioritise your interests because they are more important than you will ever know.

What are your priorities now?

What can you move away from?

What do you choose to prioritise in the future?

'Most of us spend too much time on what is urgent and not enough time on what is important.'
Stephen R. Covey

Professionalism is knowing how to do it, when to do it, and doing it.

FRANK TYGER

THINK IT

The second stage of the Knowing process is vital as it harmonises the feminine Feeling It (intuition) and the masculine Thinking It. Individually they are strong but together they are powerful.

So how do you embrace the thinking associated with *Knowing*?

It's quite simple, you ask yourself one question:

'Is this aligned with my highest potential?'

If the answer is *no* or you need to think on it, then dismiss it because when you truly *Know* then you will instantly know when something is aligned.

If you are starting out on the process of truly *Knowing* then this can be a case of trial and error. Try not to be too hard on yourself because when something is destined for you, you will attract it right back through your intentions. I will chat more on this in Book 3 of the *Life Magic* series, *The Miracle of Intent*.

For now, get to know you, what you truly want to achieve, and feel into the journey of life that you want to take. When you honour your path, those who walk alongside you in life will benefit.

Try not to overthink the **Think It** part of the process. It isn't supposed to be complicated and always remember *there is no fear in Knowing*!

Knowing and Choice

Making choices comes naturally to some people and if that's you, well done. Embracing The Power of Knowing is more about embracing the principles of the process and making them a habit, which rewires your brain and becomes less of a push and pull scenario. Of course, in any breakthrough there is always a struggle beforehand so that you learn the skills needed to break through to the next level.

If you struggle with making choices, then you need to read this chapter!

Most people do not know they have the power over their own life. Yes, of course environmental, societal and global events affect our current circumstances, but it is a choice to be a victim of circumstance or the master of your own destiny no matter what is going on in the outer world. One thing is for sure, YOU are the master of YOUR world. Whether you want to hear it or not, you are responsible for where you are right now. And you are responsible for whether you choose to see that in a positive or negative light.

We all have challenges to endure in our lifetime, many inflicted upon us by external sources. When we find peace with knowing we cannot be responsible for others' actions, we can only be responsible for our own, then there is freedom in that. We can choose to forgive others, not for them but so that we are freed from the shackles of what could have been a lifetime of pain and a lifetime lost because it was defined by a past incident. Remember, the person you look at in the mirror now stands before you warts and all. That person needs you to show up, own your choices and move forward, stepping into the power of what can be, not what was.

You can choose in any moment to learn and evolve from the shadows of the past. I promise when you choose to step into the light you will shine brighter, you will evolve from a cocoon and when you are ready to spread your wings there is a big wide world filled with opportunities for you to behold.

There is enough for everyone on this planet, there is enough for you to have anything your heart desires.

Making choices that include your desires is not selfish, it is your duty to live a life filled with things you love. So long as what you do does not intentionally harm another person then go for it, life is for living to our highest potential.

The next time you have a choice to make, ensure that you feel into it first, then ask the golden question, 'Is this aligned with my highest potential?' and if the answer is *yes*, then find the courage to take immediate action.

There is always a perception about the way you should do something; often when you truly *know* you will discover that what you are being guided to do defies conventional thought practices. It's your choice which you choose.

Knowing others is intelligence,
Knowing yourself is true wisdom.

LAO TZU

Knowing and Your Calling

'Choose a job you love, and you will never have to work a day in your life.'
Confucius

These words of Confucius ring so true to me now that I live through my passion for sharing stories with the world. This calling has seen me live a tremendous life and experience truly wonderful things that I could have only dreamed of before I took the steps forward to embark on this journey.

You see, I LOVE the journey. I love that I can get up every day and do what I love, it is kind of like I get to do my hobby every day! This got me thinking. Many people do jobs that don't fulfil them, not knowing what their calling is, or maybe not even realising that we all have a calling waiting for us to answer it. Our gift to the world is always a gift to ourselves and each gift is different. It is not a choice for our minds to make but more being open to something that presents as a possibility.

Have you ever thought on the word hobby? Do you think our hobby is actually our true calling in motion? Surely a hobby is something that fulfils us, makes us happy and something we could do all day long without watching the clock. So why do so many people choose to do a hobby in their 'spare time' as a reward for drudging through another work week? Why can't our hobbies be our jobs and our spare time be filled with hugs and time with our loved ones?

I choose the latter and have made my hobby (my calling) my job. Therefore I don't feel the need to fill my spare time with anything other than spending time with my nearest and dearest; also for walks and replenishing my energy so that I can show up as my best self, time and time again. I know I am privileged to live this life and I never take it for granted, not for one moment.

So is eradicating the unwanted job the answer we are all looking for? Do some self-discovery and make the choice for yourself. I know many people who are happy to clock in and clock out and not have to think about work again until the next time they have to clock in. That in itself is freedom. I have had those jobs in the past and they are very important jobs in society. There are many people who believe this is how things should be, when in fact that is not the case.

I invite you to think about your hobby and whether you are happy to keep it as something you do on the side, or if something more is calling you to act and upgrade your skills aligned with your passion.

Making the Choice to be Your Own Success Story

Listen to other success stories. Many of the storytellers, especially those who are connected to their divine purpose, talk about how they just *Knew* there was something they should do. Even though it defied logic they took the chance and it paid off. Yes, they had challenges to overcome but every challenge came at an integral point of their journey; a point when they were required to step up and evolve from where they were previously.

When you read such stories in their entirety you will easily identify the *Knowing* that was an integral point at the beginning of the writer's journey and then each stage along the way that required them to access their *Knowing* again. I guarantee they *felt it, thought it and actioned it*! It becomes an instant and integral part of any success story and it shows they weren't actually taking a chance at all but were aligned with actioning their highest potential. They couldn't fail once they chose to evolve through each challenge and take action through each aligned opportunity, disregarding the distractions along the way.

So how do you become your own success story? The answer is simple: you need to revisit your definition of success. I speak about this in Book 1 of this series, *The Magic of Mindfulness*. It all starts with you! Why? Because your success story may not be about how much money you have in the bank or how you build a business, your ultimate success story may be a goal or a journey or both. In Book 3, *The Miracle of Intention*, I share more on how to set and leverage intentions so they are perfectly aligned with how you navigate to your perfect destination. Right now learning how to use the Power of Knowing is important because before you set any intentions you should learn how to truly *Know*.

Part of that is to truly connect with the essence of who you are and what makes you tick. Identify what YOU want to achieve and realise that you will need to make room in your life for the magic of that to happen. Learning how to know again means you don't overthink things, you FEEL into them, that is your guide. You feel right in the depths of your soul that you want this, that this is aligned with your goals.

If you don't know your purpose just now, that is fine. If you don't know what you want to achieve, that is fine too.

What is important, and the reason I began this book with conversations with God and connecting with divine energy is because when you do, you exist on another level.

Given the level of success I have experienced to date you might be surprised to know I never knew what my purpose was until I accidentally stumbled upon it through a series of events. I believe way too much emphasis is put on the word 'PURPOSE' and there is too much stress to find what that is for us and pursue it for a lifetime.

If you focus on connecting with the divine energy within you, the power that you have to connect at a higher level in life, then you will FEEL your purpose. It is not something you think on, it is something you feel. I can quite confidently say, 'I am totally aligned with my purpose' and not because of the degrees I have or the blood, sweat, tears and thoughts I put into finding it. It all began when I got to know who I was and what made me shine from within. I can guarantee that it wasn't anything materialistic. It is always something that I connect with and that is individual.

I see so many people wasting their life pursuing success,

slogging their way through challenge upon challenge and evolving into something that is not aligned with who they truly are on the inside. They lose themselves along the way and quite often turn into someone who is not very nice to others or to themselves. That is understandable because they are living against their inner alignment. They are living through thoughts alone, not thoughts aligned with feelings, which of course is way more powerful.

One interesting fact I came across on my journey is that our heart actually has a brain and that when our intuition is actioned, that feeling we have in our gut is a combination of heart and thoughts.

No matter at what point in your life you are reading this book, if you do not feel aligned with where you are at, I invite you to consider taking an emotional break from what you are doing. Go on an inner retreat and get to know the you that once shone. Reconnect with the essence of that person. Whether you choose to stop your current life in its tracks and go on a physical destination (hello *Eat, Pray, Love*) or change your current thought cycle by introducing a practice such as meditation, yoga, walks along the beach, gratitude or whatever else works for you to begin taking steps inwards, I encourage you to embrace it. Whatever brings you to the essence of you will lead you to being successful no matter what medium it is you choose to pursue.

I have too often seen the pursuit of unaligned success resulting in many wasted years in the gift of a lifetime.

*I find comfort in knowing that I've only
lost those who didn't deserve to stay.*

RH Sin

ACTION IT

When taking action it is advised to do this through the intention of love. Loving intention is one of the fastest ways to receive what you seek.

Action It is the final part of the *Knowing* process. Taking action sets the wheels in motion. This is an important part of the process because through our actions we get a response from those around us.

Every action causes a reaction.

When actions are initiated through our power of *Knowing* we can feel confident in the decisions we are making and move forward confidently, knowing we are working towards our highest potential.

I know many people who are nervous about making decisions. Making a decision is often thought to be one of the most enormous things we do in life and yes, ultimately it is because every choice we make weaves our web of life. That is why making choices channelled through a *Knowing* will gift us the freedom to make choices that are aligned with our highest potential. Thus any setbacks or blocks come to help us grow and learn the skills we need to learn at that point to propel us forward.

Quite often people spend a lot of time covering their tracks or putting agreements in place as a precautionary measure so they won't be liable for their decisions if they prove to be wrong. And yes, I completely understand why this happens, we definitely need to protect ourselves from risk. However I believe The magical essence of the natural flow of progression and alignment is hindered in this type of scenario.

Pressing pause for a moment is fine with the flow of the Power of Knowing but when you stop and disconnect with the essence, the momentum will have been altered. And to be perfectly honest I am very passionate that when you *Know*, you *Know*. That means you learn to action things immediately if they are aligned otherwise you risk missing out on an opportunity.

Feel it, Think it, Action it.

If there is any hesitancy when you get to the stage of thinking, 'Is this aligned?' then the answer is *no*, because when you truly know, you don't hesitate. You will learn to action straight away.

The Golden Rules of Knowing

There are key rules to knowing:

1. **Honour your decisions.** Have no regrets for any decision to say no. You made the decision for a reason at that point in your life. Move on from it. If it keeps calling you back then when the time is right look into it again.
2. **Follow the three-step process.** Feel it, Think it, Action it. This should become an automatic ability and part of your daily life. Use it as part of your life ammunition when manifesting, making choices and embracing opportunities.
3. **Be at one with the essence of you.** When you do this you will be able to *Know* on a higher level and your life will automatically upgrade. You will have the opportunity to live life on your terms and aligned with who you deserve to become.
4. **Embrace the journey**. It's important to remember the value of the journey. So many people see it as a struggle, but it's not meant to be. When you are aligned the journey is an amazing experience that you never want to end. It goes on and on and the destination becomes less of a priority. This is Life Magic.

The secret to having it all is knowing that you already do.

Knowing and Taking Action on Inspired Thoughts

There are lots of lessons and wisdom paths that I have walked and many knowing stories I can share. My story about a Duchess and a publisher seems to be one that people wish to hear.

I have always had an intention to build a traditional publishing press filled with amazing established writers producing beautiful books and also creating opportunities for emerging authors. I set the intention of building a million dollar press. I am a great believer that there is miracle in intention and that when we have the right love-filled intentions ANYTHING is possible.

One night I was checking in on my Facebook family and saw that Sarah, Duchess of York was at an event in London run by a friend of mine. I loved watching her speak her words of wisdom to an audience of business owners.

It popped into my head that my son loved her Budgie the Little Helicopter books when he was younger and this led me to an inspired thought: 'I wonder if the Duchess would like to write a book for Serenity Press?'

That inspired thought set a string of actions in motion. I sat with that powerful loving intention energy and searched for the Duchess's agent. I wrote an email and it must have been passed on through the agency to the Duchess's office. I received an email requesting more information about what I was proposing and eventually a call was set up.

One of the things I promised myself was to make the process easy and not create any blocks to the flow of it. So when the call was requested during the time I was away with five of my children I still said yes. The main lesson there is to make it as simple as possible for someone to say yes.

Ask without expectation and eradicate all fear from the equation. The moment I decided to send that email I promised myself to honour the journey that would evolve and stick with it through whatever presented itself.

It was a process of trust building and showcasing my own and my team's ability to get the job done. I believe that because the Duchess and her team had an open heart and mind and we aligned very much with that, then something magical would happen — and it has.

I remember the day when I was sent through a beautifully illustrated piece of paper from the Duchess. She had sat in her garden and written about an oak tree and sent it to me. I read it and was entranced! I wanted to bring this beautiful story to life and it has quickly become *The Enchanted Oak Tree*. This book was supposed to be the first book we published because it represented so much at the time and was such an integral part of the Duchess Serenity Series project coming together.

I hope you enjoyed this insight into how by following my *Knowing* I secured a publishing deal with a Duchess. Watch this space — divine timing is in motion.

Knowing Yourself — Go Within or Go Without

When *Knowing* becomes a habit it is something you will do without having to be too mindful of it. In order to do this, you must first get to know yourself and that requires you to take time to go within.

For many people that can be a scary prospect. When we go inward, everything we haven't dealt with is there waiting for us to address it. It's important to do this regularly as we move along in our life. Those who don't can suffer major illnesses due to the festering of what is simmering inside. We all deal with things differently and when we don't honour and release the emotions we have buried during the tough times I believe they can manifest as something else.

When I moved to Australia in 2008 I did not think for one moment that I had a whole suitcase of unwanted issues tucked away. Yet so many things I had not addressed through my thirty years of living began presenting themselves one by one. It was quite overwhelming at the beginning but I then found the power in honouring and releasing them one by one. I realised that when things happen and we are not in the mindset to deal with them, we tuck them away in a special place inside until our mind and body knows we have the strength to release them. Sometimes we can resist that process because we don't feel ready but from my experience it is about stepping outside your comfort zone. It was when I did that I began to write and it was a fabulous release for me.

The best time for this process is when we are detached from the full-blown emotion and on the road to healing. Perspective is an interesting thing. We react to the way we perceive things to be and we can look at these times as a setback or a breakthrough. When the emotion is honoured (and that may be by having a good cry, hitting a punching bag or running through every aspect of the event and processing it before releasing it out of your body) I see it as a breakthrough.

I discovered the power in writing about it. Writing is an action and therefore it transfers a thought to something tangible that can be managed. Thoughts are directly connected to feelings and therefore are harder to manage. That is why when we don't feel ready, we hide them in that internal box. It is when we don't empty the box that big implosions happen.

Having grown up in Northern Ireland during the last decade of the Troubles I know there are so many internal boxes overflowing and that is why mental health is such an issue. Perhaps if resources were targeted at showing people how to empty their box or at least declutter it, then we would not have a mental health epidemic.

It is in disconnecting with our Power of Knowing that this has become such a problem. Our Power of Knowing is our internal compass, navigating us through life. When we are in tune with it then we *Know* when we need to empty our box.

So how do we reconnect? It is all about being aware of the signs, or internal call and taking the time out to stop and address whatever is happening.

Many people do this automatically but others keep suppressing the need. It is about being aware of what type of person you are.

People who are givers often keep things hidden whereas more aggressive people are constantly releasing and so their box doesn't overflow as much. Yet the anger needs to stem from somewhere so those issues still need to be addressed.

Do you ever notice that it is often the most gorgeous

people who get seriously ill?

Are you a person who releases as you go along, maybe through sports, journaling, meditating or other forms of expression? Or are you a person who brushes things under the carpet hoping that the dust blows away? But the dust doesn't blow away, it waits there building up until you take the time to address it and release it. So try to take the time to release pent up emotions. It is vital for your future health.

One of the go-to books I embrace when I feel an ailment coming on is Louise Hay's *You Can Heal Your Life*. I often mention it in my books because I believe in the science behind it. I like realising the spiritual reason for my dizziness, stomach pain, toothache or whatever is going on at any given time. That allows me to pair up medicinal treatment with self-awareness and deal with the issue from the root core. This type of self-exploration is very valuable when harnessing the power of knowing.

Knowing removes all fear.

KAREN MCDERMOTT

KNOWING MUSINGS

Knowing in Embracing Adversity

When life isn't going how you hoped it would it is often an impulsive reaction to feel down and low in spirit and your sparkle dims. We all go through low points in life. It is these low points that help us on the journey to the high points and lead us to treasure those better times and be grateful when we are in them. *Knowing* is also key to embracing those periods when it is not a time for action but a time to be still.

Remember, it is as important to stop on your journey and rest your soul as it is to keep moving forward. If you are a person who doesn't take time to rest you will often be confronted with obstacles that will stop you in your tracks. And should you not embrace the opportunity to be still you will keep being confronted with bigger and more powerful obstacles until you do become more aligned.

I wrote this chapter as the world is going through a global pandemic. I observed as the shock of it all rippled through the globe that this Corona virus was spreading to countries regardless of their wealth. I observed how fear consumed our every moment and life changed in an instant. The first week was one of the longest weeks as uncertainty was lingering in the air, people were panic buying in the shops (I don't want to mention the T word) all in a bid to be prepared for what was to come.

I took actions that I felt I needed to take. I pulled my kids out of school and simplified our life. I limited the number of times I left the house, set up an outdoor office for me and a home-schooling table for my four girls and got on with being. I could have been consumed with the sensationalised news that pulsated from the TV screen from dawn to dusk but I chose to keep myself updated but not let it consume our every thought. I chose to focus on what I could do rather than what I couldn't. This perspective alone ensures that when we come out the other end of this, my family's experience will not be a harrowing nightmare.

I want it to be that time when we all got to be together. The time when we looked out for each other, when I prayed that my family in my home and overseas would be kept safe and that through my choices I helped to flatten the curve and save lives. In week two things shifted, a unitedness started to blanket the globe, people were sharing love-filled quotes and random acts of kindness were happening. Love was starting to prevail. One perspective that touched me was a picture of the abandoned city of Paris with the caption, *'This is not a picture of abandonment, this is a picture of love, the love that our world has for each other that they are willing to stay indoors for one another.'*

I share the story about the pandemic because we can all relate, this is something that will go down in the history books. Currently we are still going through it. But the lesson in this shines bright, even though what is happening is harrowing on so many levels and I feel blessed to be writing this without having any fatalities in my family. However I do see it as being about perspective and how you choose to embrace a situation that has been imposed on you. We didn't choose to have a global pandemic but when you live with the ability to *Know*, you can have faith in the knowing that you will be guided towards the next step.

I feel blessed to not be consumed with fear. I am glad I chose to be filled with faith that I will be guided through it, and that I trust my instinct to make what I feel are the best choices. Yes, everything will change, but it will be an incremental transition from this point, the shocker is behind us. We will all adjust. Things will not be the same. They can't be as the mindset of a whole generation has been adjusted. But what if this new beginning allows us to rebirth into a more connected way of being rather than the disconnected ways of before? The collective choice will be that of humanity in 2020. I will continue to make my choices in the hope they inspire others to also make more aligned choices.

Knowing and Embracing Different Practices

Have you ever heard of Sankalpa? I have discovered that I love this practice and in fact have been practising it for many years without even knowing it.

I love it because when you delve deeper into the understanding of it all, the roots are deeply embedded in harmonising science to make life magic happen.

Wikipedia defines Sankalpa as *'an intention formed by the heart and mind — a solemn vow, determination, or will. In practical terms a Sankalpa means a one-pointed resolve to focus both psychologically and philosophically on a specific goal. Sankalpa is a tool meant to refine the will, and to focus and harmonise mind and body.'*

When I discovered this definition I shared it with my beautiful community, most of whom were familiar with the concept but not the name. It is refreshing to discover that more and more amazing people are embracing these ways of setting intentions because intentions are so much more powerful when sourced through our root core.

Have you explored Mysticism?

Mysticism has recently caught my attention. My thoughts and energies seem aligned in this realm of consciousness and as I am a curious person when it comes to things that strike an intrigue in me I have chosen to explore it further. Had I been born a couple of hundred years ago I may have been burnt at a stake for this curiosity but I am blessed to live in an era where I can openly pursue these interests.

'True mystics simply open their souls to the oncoming wave. Sure of themselves, because they feel within them something better than themselves, they prove to be great men of action, to the surprise of those for whom mysticism is nothing but visions, and raptures and ecstasies.'

Henri Bergson

Going a bit deeper here on the topic of Knowing and Mysticism I discovered there are three major aspects of Mysticism.

1. Practical Understanding
2. Spirit.
3. Superstition

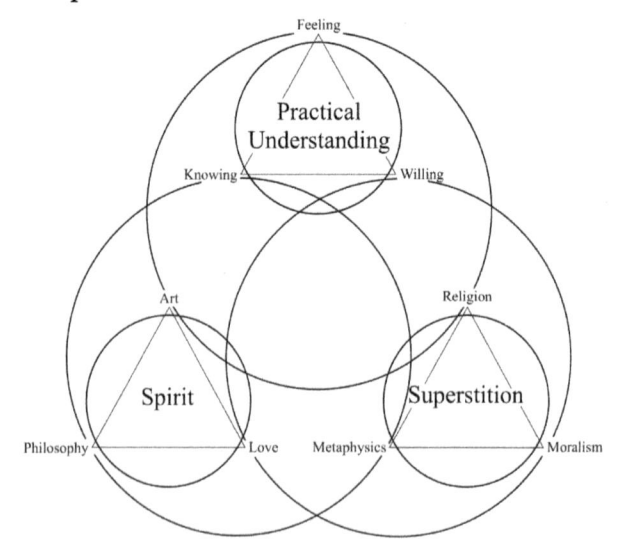

[Diagram: Three overlapping circles labeled "Practical Understanding" (with vertices Feeling, Knowing, Willing), "Spirit" (with vertices Art, Philosophy, Love), and "Superstition" (with vertices Religion, Metaphysics, Moralism).]

Source: Wikipedia

Knowing is part of practical understanding and connected to the components of Will and Feelings.

Closely connected to the outer aspect of Spirit are Love, Philosophy and Art. I find that when I embrace art, love and philosophical ideologies my body pulsates at a heightened level. It is a bizarre feeling that I have become familiar with because quite often what follows is something powerful. Something truly connected with the essence of my soul. I love the fact that these three components are pinnacles of the aspect of Spirit.

And the final aspect of Superstition has me excited. Being of Irish heritage I grew up with superstitions and am of course familiar with the components of metaphysics, moralism and religion.

I love that LOVE is a huge part of mysticism. It is at the core, it lives through it. I am a great believer that God is found in love and when we learn to truly love ourselves, another and life then we are living through God's will. Love is the most powerful force of all. Nothing can defeat a strong-willed and true loving intention.

I would like to share some of my thoughts on Religion but first here are some definitions from the Oxford Dictionary.
1. *The belief in and worship of a superhuman controlling power, especially a personal God or gods.*
2. *A particular system of faith and worship.*
3. *A pursuit or interest followed with great devotion.*

There are different definitions of religion. What I want to highlight is that religion is a choice we make in a belief system. My problem with some religions is that we are not giving the choice, either through our inherited beliefs or imposed beliefs because of circumstance. This led me to many years of not truly relating to a religion and yet still having a good connection to what I felt was Godly energy. I love unconditionally, I live through love and I have my own little rituals that allow me to connect with divine energy so that I can project loving energy and thoughts to those I love whether they be near or far. In turn I live a blessed life and approach any challenges as lessons and opportunities to grow in ability and spirit. I am in tune with who I am and feel blessed that I can say that with conviction. The problem is I want EVERYONE to feel this way too. I know that if everyone gave themselves permission to get to know who they truly are they would have an authentic deep-rooted connection with God.

God lives through us all individually. We achieve a divine connection to the almighty energy when we do the hard work of getting to know ourselves. Most people don't know and sadly may never know what I am talking about but if you are reading this and you don't know the feeling of a divine connection, please know that you CAN have it. It is within everyone's reach. The journey to this space may be a bit messy but when you reach the destination there is no going back. This is what I have discovered on my journey and in researching this book I was surprised to read in *The Art of Mysticism by Gabriyell Sarom* that my thoughts and practices are echoed in this book. I was delighted to learn that when embraced it is a shortcut to the Divine we all crave, and that this divinity is found through defining our own personal connection with God.

I look forward to sharing more of my aligned discoveries and interpreting them in my perspective for you throughout this and my other books in the series.

However, I do invite you to explore your relationship with yourself because the closer you are to your authentic connection to divine energy, the stronger your power of knowing will be.

Creativity is allowing yourself to make mistakes. Art is knowing which ones to keep.

SCOLL ADAMS

Knowing and the Essence of Faith

'God is within us all.'
LK 17:1

I know this is a bit out there in relevance to how the world thinks of God and in speaking this way I am open to criticism but hear me out.

I believe we overcomplicate God. I believe God is an almighty source, a collective energy that is dominant in our world and in all worlds. I believe we all have the gift of God within us and what we put out collectively from within congregates in the external to create the energy by which we are all governed. It is important that we realise this and start owning the actions we take and the energy we share with the world. It is this energy that we collectively project out into the world that creates our external experiences.

Isaac Newton's third law, the law of motion, states that *'from every action there is a reaction.'* It is both science and a valid theory as the Bible states, *'Be not deceived; God is not mocked: for whatsoever a man soweth, that shall he also reap.'* Galatians 6:7-9

Many people really don't want the pressure of the power they have within, they prefer someone else to handle that responsibility as it is too much to comprehend. When I first watched *The Secret* by Rhonda Byrne I got so excited by the potential of the possibilities being opened up to by my mind. Infinite thoughts were exciting to me, whereas my sister did not feel the same way. A gentler approach through Louise Hay's *You Can Heal Your Life* was a wonderful introduction to the possibilities and how by adjusting our thought patterns we can influence our external and internal life. How do you feel about having ownership over your experience of life through your thoughts?

The good news is, we can only be responsible for our own inner God. Yes, we can connect in a positive way with others and that reflects on the outer world we experience — both our immediate world that we choose to surround ourselves with and also the bigger picture global world of which we are a part.

If you want to do something to save our world then the best place to start is within ourselves. The more people going within and getting themselves in a happy place in life, the more we all benefit. So do us all a favour and find your 'happy' because the world needs it.

I was asked to reflect on MY relationship with God and it is simple. I am my own God, you are your own God. God is a divine energy that impacts us all whether we choose to embrace it or not. We serve our God best by getting to know our strengths and weaknesses, finding our true purpose in life and reconnecting with humanity. Choose good over bad, choose happiness over sadness, know that your contribution to the world is just as important as ANY other person's.

Alone we can do a lot but together we can do so much more!

This is why goodwill communities are needed in our world. People coming together with a collective intention to do good. This is all the more powerful when each of those people begins with doing good for themselves because then they can give their best to others. It can be facilitated online, in person or any other way. For me, my Life Magic community and this collection of books is my gift to the world; it is me doing my bit to raise a positive vibration so that my world and the world of others is enhanced.

Some of the biggest problems in the world can be solved by first taking the step to find our purpose. Yours may be being the best mum in the world, which may bring you so much joy that you need never do anything else for decades. That unconditional love will not only nourish you, it will also nourish your children to become the best version of themselves.

For me two wrongs never make a right, so it is important to take a moment to consider the source of someone's anger. You may realise that in their circumstances you would not act much differently. Quite often people with rage just want to be heard, to share the root of their frustration and for someone to actually care enough to help them find a solution.

Yes, there are learned beliefs that are hard to break through but realise I said hard, not impossible. When the intention is to find a solution, anything is possible. An example of this is my experience of growing up in Northern Ireland where there was a religious war going on. Soldiers walked the streets, bombs would go off at unpredictable times and the energy was intense at times. Each person believed wholeheartedly in the mission of the side they were born into; horrible things happened to some families that engraved a harsh memory into their family history. I too have memories that I would rather forget, but there is no freedom in forgetting. Freedom is only gifted in forgiveness. Look at the example of Jesus; he forgave but the other side didn't and they have had to bear the cross of that ever since. Imagine if Julius Ceasar had had a change of heart, set his ego aside for a time and forgiven Jesus for what he obviously felt strongly about.

We value life more than we did then when rulers were

not held accountable for their actions as they are now in most cases. Ultimately my point is that we can do our bit for the world by doing our bit for ourselves because that goodness ripples across the globe. As long as more and more people choose to, with the truest of intentions, serve themselves first and others through that intention, then miracles can happen. (We explore this in more depth in the next book, *The Miracle in Intention*.)

Please know that I am not on any campaign to change your religious beliefs. I merely wish to share with you my perspective on God and what I interpret to be the message of God.

I have many years of reading and research planned to explore and enhance my *Knowing* around this subject but for now I believe religion entrenched itself in so much of our history because it gave people hope. It gave them a safe haven from the cruelty of the outside world; from those who didn't embrace goodness, who were fuelled by motivations other than living through loving intention.

For me God is LOVE.

I want to share with you a story…

I have always genuinely cared about others. It's in my DNA. I have always been taught to put myself first and as my mother says, 'If it makes you happy and doesn't hurt someone else then go for it, you have my support.'

Growing up in this type of environment, one where it was safe to be curious and explore MY life has been a true blessing. I could discover myself and what I wanted to experience in my lifetime. We are here for a lifetime, not an eternity but our legacy will impact future generations. For me, I love to achieve, I love to experience new things, my zest for life is filled with curiosity. When I am passionate about something it is my personal endeavour to pursue achievement and discover a new way. I don't have fear surrounding the outcome. In fact, I bring people along for the ride who are curious too, so that they can embrace the magic of exploring something that is unknown.

Back to the story…

I was guided to a beautiful all-knowing person who chooses to be connected to energies that are no longer in physical form so that her clients' personal questions can be answered.

I was so busy in my publishing world with all the projects I had on the go and knew I wasn't taking the time to open up to my inner guide. I was missing something important. When the thought came that I should connect with Rebecca because there was something I needed to know, I knew something huge was waiting for me to embrace it.

During our chat I asked about my writing and if it was going to reach the audience I hoped it would. And I watched as the answer flowed through to me: *'You need to explore your relationship with God. There is something there that is a block but it is waiting hidden for you to uncover it and share it with the world. This is actually huge, something that hasn't been uncovered before.'* Instantly I knew that was why we needed to chat.

There are many religions staking claim to God but I choose to think of God as Love. The ability to love myself and my neighbour, to genuinely care and share my personal gifts with the world. I believe our quest is to find our purpose and to build our personal world aligned with that because when enough of us find our purpose and serve ourselves and the world through that energy, it is almighty and powerful and will ripple across our globe.

Afterwards I went out for coffee with a friend who is very connected to God but when I left that catch up I felt compelled to share something with her ...

For me it's simple: God is Love. Love is the greatest power of all, a divine force that is within us all. There is nothing as strong as when love combines. It is in us all, around us all and in everything we do. When we embrace love, it grows, it nourishes, and it enriches life and nature. When we don't love, things start to disintegrate, destabilise and decompose. That's why I come from a heart space as much as possible. The more of us who do this will all make the world we live in a Godlier place for us and our future generations.

Why is this important to *Knowing*? It is a big responsibility to know that God is within us all. It is easier to think that God is something higher than us, another entity that we access and who has got our back when we need it. The idea of this divine source being within us and that we can choose through our actions whether to live in faith or fear is a huge responsibility for those of us who have become accustomed to being guided by others and feel safe in that. And yet that trust that many have placed in others has quite often been taken advantage of by those in positions of power. What the world needs is more of us getting to know and love ourselves, and in turn we will be able to give the best of ourselves to others. *'Love your neighbour as yourself.' There is no commandment greater than this. Mark 12:21*

I am not here to Bible bash, I did religious studies at school and grew up a Catholic so I have absorbed some of the teachings. I have come to realise the Bible is a book of infinite wisdom, a book back into ourselves, not a book that is to be projected outward. It is a story. I live with a strong sense of the power in the written word to not only reach the hearts and minds of people in our current lives, but also offer a legacy of thoughts for future generations to learn from.

I believe that we don't truly understand the Bible until we truly understand ourselves. Our biggest gift to humanity is to get to know what makes us tick and live through that with passion and purpose.

We should read this book of divine wisdom at a stage of our lives where we are able to connect with ourselves, fall in love with who we are as a person and what we have to offer the world. As with everything else in life, we should extract what resonates with our soul and incorporate that into our lives.

The Bible is for everyone, but not everyone will connect with the same wisdom held within and that is perfectly okay. I do believe that within the words in this almighty book there are the answers to OUR heart's desires and all of our problems. It is a book that can be interpreted in many ways but so can life. The stories we tell ourselves are our masters because our beliefs fuel our actions. That is okay when our beliefs are aligned with our values and our purpose but when they are not we can become misaligned and that is not good for anyone.

We evolve, thoughts evolve, behaviours evolve and humanity evolves. I believe that going within to give the best to those outside of ourselves is very important. It is not about sacrificing ourselves for others. It is about having enough for ourselves and sharing with those less fortunate so that they can find the light within themselves and shine it onto another.

Kindness is filled with light.

*The best way of knowing a person
is to love them without expectation.*

KP Weaver

Knowing to Heal

Have you ever heard stories from healers? They are everyday people who have the ability to activate healing from within a person. I know I have an ability to heal. Being a mum of six, I know the power love has to heal anything from a grazed knee to a 40-degree temp. I have been there through those scary moments. I also know what it is like to heal myself. I have had certain ailments that I have healed through alternative remedies. I believe in medicine but I also believe in not being totally reliant on it as we have more ability to heal ourselves than we give ourselves credit for, and we turn to over the counter medicine way too easily.

When you know yourself, your nearest and dearest and even when you get to know someone in need, it is amazing how you can channel into their healing need. Quite often ailments stem from emotional issues that have not been dealt with so when you take the time to find the root of the problem and do some inner work in relation to that, it is amazing the healing that can take place. There is a reason why some people experience certain illnesses and others don't. It's how we process things and quite often it is the good people who suffer because they are the ones that take on other people's burdens. It's a sad and often unfair reality. Whereas someone who might have abused their body over the span of their lifetime will not, they will have other ailments, probably physical.

Louise Hay's book *You Can Heal Your Life* will help you understand the root cause of any illness.

Currently, as I write this book I have a stomach issue. I have NEVER had a stomach issue in my life and when I checked Louise's book to find out the emotional issue behind stomach problems, it all makes sense. So how do I take control of the situation and address the problem? Aligned affirmations are an amazing resource to use, they ease your brain into connecting with the root cause, increase healing potential and speed up the process.

The Knowing in Writing

I have worked in the publishing industry for many years. I have also been writing for a number of years and with both of these influences in my life I rotate in writing circles and interact with writers regularly. One thing I have observed is that authors set the intention and then the story they are to write reveals itself. It comes from a seedling of an idea. For those writers who trust the process of *Knowing* (feel it, think it, action it), their books evolve into something that stands out.

A *Knowing* when it comes to writing is when a writer is open to the natural evolutionary journey of story. For fiction it is allowing the characters permission to grow into themselves with freedom to navigate their own story.

There is power in a word. The power to inspire, to comfort, to heal. Words can entertain and even change the world. Reading allows for interdimensional transcending. Words flow through an author and when they find their way to a reader who needs to read them at that very moment they can be transformative. Becoming a fine author does not happen overnight as there are certain skills to attain. However, the ability to connect and flow a story through to a page is something that is on a higher vibration than anything academic therefore belief in your ability to write is merely a limited belief that needs to be lifted. I hear it all of the time 'I can't write' these words are often said without much thought, they are a belief. I am of the belief that if you can communicate with others through words or sign you can write, as it is just another form of communication. Please don't get me wrong I know what it takes to write a good book, especially a fictional novel, I am just trying to emphasis that so many people block themselves from the possibility of putting pen to paper even when they have so much to give the world through the written word.

I can say this as my first novel, albeit not a literary masterpiece came through me feeling passionate about sharing a message with the world, being open to the possibility of the opportunity to do so coming to me, and then actioning it when it arrived. This all happened in two days. When the epiphany came I wrote a blog post but that wasn't enough so I set an intention to write a book. Then I saw that a challenge called NaNoWriMo (National Novel Writing Month) was beginning, so I signed up and for thirty days I wrote 1667 words each day. By the end of the month I had a 50,000 word novel.

I have shared this story many times but it is important as it shows what can be achieved when you set an intention and stay true to your *Knowing*. It was the most impractical time for me to consider writing a novel. I had a new baby and two other kids at home with me but it ended up being one of the best decisions I ever made as it set me on a path where I now live my purpose every day.

I will continue to improve my writing skills, *Knowing* I have the ability to make it happen when I set the intention. Intention and *Knowing* are a powerful combination.

When you have set an intention and are focused on a goal you will work hard to achieve success. It is important to remain connected to your *Knowing* when it comes to balancing the other key elements of your life, which are Love and Life. When you remain connected to your *Knowing* it will let you know when certain areas need your focus and when you need to direct attention to them.

*Forgive yourself for not knowing what
you didn't know before you learned it.*

A Group Knowing Conversation

Conversations are glorious, they lead to all sorts of gold so I have to share with you all a conversation I had in my Life Magic Facebook group (which you are invited to join).

KNOWING

WHAT DO YOU BELIEVE KNOWING TO BE?

Hi Life Magicians, I am finishing off my next book The Power of Knowing and thought it would be nice to write a chapter about what other people perceive *Knowing* to be.

Would you like to share with me below what you think or feel when you hear the word *Knowing*?

Tanya Southey

I have seen so many sunsets. Sunsets that the Highveld in South Africa is renowned for. Where the colours are unashamedly bright, and the sky flaunts glory to all who will take the time out to stand in wonder. The birds would swoop against the sunset, tiny sparrows, flying joy against the painted backdrop and the crickets would get out their violins to start the symphony of the night. I am not sure why I remember this particular sunset. I was waiting outside for my dad to come home. I was allowed to wander between our house, the Mitchell's and the Williamson's who lived on either side, beyond that the boundary was a no go zone as the sun retreated behind

We invariably fell off, especially me, who was never the most athletic of the crew. This particular evening, I put the universe to the test and slowly put one foot in front of the other and balance my way from the edge of our property to the edge of the Williamson's, the sun beckoning me to believe in myself, to believe that I was here for a purpose, for a reason, for growth for the good of myself and the world. As I made it to the end, I felt my spirit expand. Those last gingered steps where I could have fallen off and didn't. Those seconds that confirmed that what I was feeling was in fact the truth. Here I was, the length of the property, done, I had made it. What I felt was right. I never told anyone of that experience as a child. I had no words to articulate or explain it, but I felt that universe had blessed me and that I was going to be something. What I did not realise was that feeling where I felt so filled with power and creativity and the ability to do something would also clash with everything I was being programmed for at a societal and social level. I was just a girl. A girl who was supposed to get married, stay small, have babies, be a good mum and host tea parties and dinner parties for a successful husband.

Kez Wickham St George
Knowing, a concept some find it hard to understand. Those of us that do know the magic of that feeling deep in your gut it's right for you or maybe not for you. It's that 3 way conversation between tum, heart & head, Trusting your god given magic your on the right road , being authentically you.

Michelle Weitering

For me.

Knowing is a feeling...that gives me goosebumps. positive, knowing goosebumps. My antena for great things that are emerging...

It's a complete trust in myself, that no matter the situation.. If it feels right, it will all work out right, no matter.

To know is to know. To feel. To trust your gut.

Susan Wakefield

Mona Lisa smiles at me in that omniscient, all-knowing way. I search her eyes past grey and foreboding Paris skies; I have not seen the light of day since this bathroom became my polished tile prison cell of sorts, locked away as I have been from life and reality and me. I am finally out, set free to the sublime taste of fresh finds and wind upon my lips; I waste no time and go directly to her. We have not seen each other for months since my confinement from the World's order; yet I know when our eyes meet again we are full of this quiet, unobtrusive thing called Knowing. From behind her bullet-proof glass we meet the trade secrets, understanding destinies, shared trajectories as our paths cross and stars shine, crashing in symphonic timpani and understand in the prescient here and now. I humbly bow and receive all of the messages meant for me across a thousand seas, the map upon which my knowing guide and I will follow the tides to navigate me safely to arrive again upon the shores of myself. I am home.

Susan Wakefield, Excerpt from Decency.

Skylar J Wynter
When I hear of or experience "knowing" it is innate. It is seated deep within and there is never any "questioning" creating noise around it. It is truth rooted in the bedrock of something more divine than my thoughts or physical body. There is no escaping it. Acceptance is the only course of action.

Lisa Thompson
Knowing that I can achieve anything I want .
    Knowing that I have the power to be the master of my own destiny

Barbara Gurney
Knowing that being me is enough

Jean Frost
Knowing for me is something that you do without hesitation. Knowing is an instinct deep within. A feeling of yes and no. Prickles on the skin.

Jodie Elizabeth
Knowing is a deep seated inner feeling in your gut. Instinctive, first thought - innate sense within. It feels right.

Enisa Haines
Knowing for me is an inner instinct and something more. Something from outside of me, a higher source, that I have somehow tapped into that guides my inner instinct and feelings.

Jayme Ahern
Knowing is a constant battle between what we are taught, what we are told and what we feel. What we 'know' is always decided by these three factors.

Sonja Rupnik
Knowing its my thoughts and feelings that determines my paths on life...easy or hard

Monique Alexandra
If knowledge is external, factual and finite, knowing has an infinite, deep inner source. To me, knowing is something not easily explained because it just IS. It comes upon as when we least expect it, bringing insight, wisdom, and sometimes a little nudge that maybe you didn't really want to hear. But if you listen and trust, knowing can guide you where you need to go in a more fulfilling way than if you just do what you should, or what has always been done before.

Suzanne Therese Costello
The prickly feeling I get, tiny tingles along my arms & slowly creeping up to my neck. They come & go so quickly, fleetingly & could be missed except they have happened many times before. The recognition that I feel them every time someone tells me something profound. That tingle tells me that the words are the truth. Knowing is knowing. ♥

Amanda Schubert
Knowing is easy. It is like sinking into a warm bath, at once weightless yet all-encompassing. Your soul feels light and it's as though time is simultaneously speeding up and slowing down.

In that moment, everything just IS, without that niggling urge to question or to pick-apart the how, or why, or what if. It is Knowing. It is home.

Sally Newman

Knowing; is embracing your own truth.

Understanding the thoughts that guide you; accepting the thoughts that challenge you and responding to the thoughts that empower you.

Knowing is truth.

Not truth in words.

Not truth in numbers

But truth in your own existence.

Kelly Van Nelson

Knowing is wholeheartedly trusting yourself and your instincts because there is an unwavering belief in them at that given moment

Linda Blackshaw

For me knowing is an inner sensation felt in the solar plexus and heart center that I'm to go a particular way or make a particular choice.no doubts a quiet acceptance yet excitement too to go for it. Or when the knowing is no then there is a clear message don't do it then I can let it go with no doubts or what ifs. When I think about it I open up my channels to Source and trust. As the saying goes Trust your gut feeling.

Lisa Benson

Knowing for me is the inner guidance you cannot ignore. A sense that you know exactly what is right for you, or what you need to do in a situation even there's no proof. When you deviate from this guidance, you may take a detour, but you'll eventually come back to this 'knowing.' It is a feeling we learn to trust.

Holly Holland Rogoschewsky
Knowing is effortless. It is simply there, comfortable and ready for you to move forward with without hesitation.

Veronica Gypsy
Knowing to me is an incredible sense of flow that takes over, with inner soul clarity, but sometimes unnoticed like a sacred secret. Like a perfect fit, like you would imagine a 1950's soft leather glove worn till its moulded uniquely to one's hand, or like the stars alignment that have been directing the world since the start of time. Like it just is.

Knowing for me is a rare awareness especially if you are so blocked by the external, but the minute I began to give attention to my truth, then the universe began to wrap me in my own tune, my own wave & precious resonance. When I am in harmony with this divine meaning that links with this innate knowing, then I know I am on my own unique meant to be path & all is bliss.

*The most difficult thing in life
is to know yourself.*

THALES

KNOWING STORIES

Knowing with Joanne Fedler

'I want to get off this plane.'

Zed looked at me with wide eyes. 'You're kidding, right?'

I wasn't. My heart was kicking in my ribcage. A shrill squeal pierced my ears. I could feel the sweat under my neck.

'We're not meant to go.'

Zed closed his eyes and sank his head into his heads.

'It's just a technical problem – they're fixing it.'

But it wasn't just that. We had been on the runway for forty-five minutes waiting for aeroplane engineers to fix the problem our pilot had said 'wouldn't take long to sort out and we'll be in the air soon.'

My impatience aside, this was not the first, but the third huge delay to our long-awaited trip to Tasmania – the honeymoon the two of us had been waiting for, for twenty years. In the past four weeks, two other major disruptions had stalled our plans. Zed was involved in a massive business deal that threatened to roll over into our precious ten days away. We'd only been given the all clear in the past forty-eight hours. We'd packed with such relief that we were going to get to have our honeymoon after all.

But then the night before we were meant to fly out at 6am the following morning, our kitten Archie suddenly got violently ill. We found ourselves at an emergency vet at 11pm. They couldn't find anything obviously wrong with him, gave him an injection and told us that if he wasn't better by morning, to bring him back.

At 4am when we woke up to get ready for the airport, I took one look at Archie and said to Zed, 'He's not well, how can we go away and leave him?'

Zed had sighed. 'It's okay, we'll go on another honeymoon.'

I loved him so much in that moment as we drove Archie back to the vet, watching our 6am flight and our ten-day campervan trip slip away forever.

The vet took x-rays and hydrated Archie. By 10am he said, 'We'll keep him for a few days for observation, but this cat is going to be fine. You should go on your holiday.'

Our daughter arranged to pick Archie up from the vet in a few days and Zed bought new tickets for later that afternoon.

Now we were on the plane that was due to fly out at 2pm.

Except it was now 3pm and there was still a technical problem with the aeroplane.

'It's not safe to fly,' I said to Zed.

To prove my point, I took out my pendulum from my bag and I whispered, 'Is it safe to fly to Tasmania?'

The pendulum swung, 'No.'

'See? See?' I said to Zed.

'You're going to make us get off this plane because a &*^% pendulum swings horizontally instead of vertically?'

It wasn't because of the pendulum. The pendulum had just confirmed what I already knew to be true – we weren't meant to be on this plane. It was the third 'sign'. I tried to explain this to Zed, but frankly, he was over it.

'If we get off this plane, that's it. We are not going to Tasmania – not later, not tomorrow. We're going home and we're going to forget about this honeymoon.'

He was as exhausted and disappointed as I was. Except I knew we had to get off this plane.

'I'm sorry,' I whispered. I wondered if I was being ridiculous. I felt bad for Zed. Maybe I was just a mad wife.

Zed called the air stewardess over. 'I'm sorry but my wife

wants to get off the plane,' he said with exasperation.

'Really? The problem should be sorted out soon,' she assured us.

The peer pressure was crushing. People around us were starting to pay attention.

Suddenly the captain's voice rumbled through the cabin.' Apologies once again folks for the delay. The problem has been sorted out. We'll be in the air as soon as we can.'

'What do you want to do?' Zed asked.

I sighed. All my instincts were yelling at me, but I now felt stupid. Was I being irrational? Was I just sleep deprived? Anxious for no reason?

'Okay,' I said, trying to hide my terror.

I sat back in my seat and closed my eyes, trying to calm myself down. Zed reached for my hand. I pulled away. I didn't want him to touch me.

The engines revved. I tried to focus on my breathing. I tried to meditate. I tried not to think about the past twenty-four hours. I tried to think of happy things. How wonderful Tasmania would be – just me and Zed in a campervan for ten days. It had never been just the two of us. But my nerves ????

The engines continued to rev. And rev. And rev. After twenty minutes, they stopped. The captain's voice came over the loudspeaker again. 'I'm really sorry ladies and gents, it seems the problem hasn't been quite sorted out... we're just getting the technicians on board, please sit back, relax and we'll have this sorted out in no time.'

Then Zed turned and said, 'Okay, okay.'

He summoned the air stewardess and let her know we wanted to get off the plane.

'It's going to cause a further delay to all the passengers

because we have to find your baggage.'

'I'm sorry,' he said, 'but my wife doesn't want to fly.'

She shrugged but I could see the thought bubble above her head: '...*seriously, some people...*'

We grabbed our hand luggage and did the walk of shame down the aisle with every passenger's eyes boring into our backs. As soon as they opened the cabin door and I stepped back into the tunnel leading to the terminal, my whole body relaxed.

Zed was furious. He was cold and silent as we walked all the way back to the gate where an airport assistant asked us for our names so they could start looking for our bags.

I stood next to him, ashamed, upset. What had I just done? I'd sabotaged our honeymoon. I'd made us get off a plane. Who does that? What sort of lunatic actually voluntarily disembarks from a plane?

We must have been standing there for no more than five minutes, when suddenly we heard a commotion – and all the other passengers began to emerge from the tunnel. The captain had just ordered everyone off the plane.

It clearly wasn't safe to fly to Tasmania.

This time Zed turned to me, his eyes wide. 'How did you know?'

I shrugged. I just knew. I didn't need a technician or the captain to tell me.

In the world we live in, people trust facts. We talk of 'knowing' something if we've researched a topic. If there's evidence to support a view. Once we've spent enough time with someone, we may be qualified to say, *I know her.* Knowing equals certainty and certainty requires proof; prior history, experience. How might you know whether a cancer treatment

*You are very powerful, providing you
know how powerful you are.*

YOGI BHAJI

works? What it's like to immigrate? To be a woman of colour? The grief of losing a parent? If you can say, 'been there, done that.'

There is no magic in this knowing. It's a mathematical equation, a qualification: if you have enough knowledge to back up your view, you 'know' and few would argue your ignorance.

What is far more interesting is whether we can *know* something or someone without this history? Can we ever say, *I know this to be true*, or *I know how to do this* or *I know he would never behave like that* when we encounter a situation, fact or person for the first time? Can we say *I know it is not safe to be on this plane in the absence of the captain telling us to disembark?*

This calls us into the energetics of something we don't usually refer to as 'knowing'. We may refer to it as a 'gut feeling', 'hunch', or 'intuition', words we tend to associate with ditzy folk who burn incense, walk around barefoot and live on coconut water for thirty days to 'cleanse'.

But in the past few decades, science has begun to catch up with mysticism. We now have 'proof' that quantum physics – entanglement, or what Einstein referred to as 'spooky action at a distance', where our thoughts, emotions and energies impact on the physical universe, is real. Rainer Maria Rilke, the German philosopher and poet wrote 'The future enters us long before it happens'. This, I believe is both quantum and a very simple 'knowing', It's not being psychic. It's not about 'reading the future', it's about discerning an outcome in the absence of any prior experience or any reason to expect the result other than a 'feeling' or a 'belief that it is so'.

I can't remember when I first knew I was born for a reason,

but I spent my childhood with a kind of precocious clarity that whatever I was here for was important. The world felt like a painful place – an astrologer I once consulted confirmed that it was a difficult decision for me to come here. That brought tears to my eyes. I had a loving family, but happiness felt far from reach in a world cleft by injustice and unfairness. I certainly didn't want the goodies in life if not everyone could have them too. For a time, this made me a self-hating white Jewish woman. Until an African American friend at Yale told me to make peace with who I was, because 'nobody trusts self-hating politics'.

I knew I could have anything I wanted – I don't know if this stemmed from my privilege, or from something else deep inside. I knew I could study overseas, become a lawyer, a judge, a politician, an author. I even knew I could have any relationship I wanted – not because I am anything of a great beauty – far from it (my dad once told me to stop dieting because I'd never be a model, 'look at that nose, those thighs…' – he meant this with love, not judgement), but because I understood that people would be drawn to me for something that had nothing to do with my appearance. Whatever about me was special at times felt deep in my head (the way I thought), or in my chest (the way I felt). I always trusted that part of me. At times I thought of it as my charisma, my personality, my heart. It's the part of me that cares about the world, that cries at the pain of people I love or even strangers. It has always been the truest part of me.

At twenty, when I went on my first Buddhist meditation retreat, it got a name. My teachers spoke of the *timeless, ageless aspects of self*, the higher self, the dimensions that transcend personality, ego, experience or circumstance. It was always the part of me that carried what I now can name as my 'knowing'. Some call it intuition. Some call it self-belief, self-esteem or integrity.

When you have a rich inner life as I always have, it becomes a refuge. I would snuggle here to escape the pain of the world around me, the way some people get swallowed into books. The Bronte sisters, I once read, lived between realities – their imaginary world and their day to day lives. At times, I felt this way too – I would seek out my own thoughts, imagination and dreams. I wanted to know what my dreams meant. I replayed them in my head by day long before I had read a single book about the power of the subconscious mind and the messages our dreams carry for us.

I have also always trusted creativity – the ability to make something from nothing. My father was a cartoonist and so I spent my childhood watching as he would take a blank piece of paper and within minutes, he'd create a world on it – a dragon breathing fire, a princess in a castle, a black panther leaping through the jungle. As a writer, I know the feeling of taking the seed of an idea and putting words on a page until you have a book, a story, a universe people can enter into. This magical quality is available to everyone, some of us just know how to use it.

I have called on this knowing throughout my life – it roared when Zed, a friend of mine told me 'I was the one he wanted to spend the rest of his life with', it arrived in my dream one night when branches grew from my breasts, out my t-shirt and reached for the sky (days later I discovered I was pregnant); I trusted it when we decided to immigrate from South Africa to Australia – a place I had never visited and which wasn't even on my holiday list; I have tuned into it every time I have started writing a book; I let it guide me when I decided to split up from a business partner and become a full-time author though she tried to convince me of the folly of relying on the unknown when I may never 'make it'. I honoured it when I chose in 2014 to invest in a business course that drained my life savings.

I follow its guidance whenever I am unsure. And I use it every single day of my life to make the thousand business decisions I need to – what colour to use, what font to go for, who to hire, who to place my confidence in. When I facilitate workshops and retreats, I tune into my knowing, and ask for guidance to say the right thing, offer the perfect insight, and get out of the way of what the group needs me for. I place myself into this knowing each day when I ask for guidance, when I pray to be 'an instrument of divine grace and love in all I think, do and say'.

I've used it to determine if my child is really in danger or whether I am being irrationally neurotic. I've quietened into it to make the impossible decision to euthanise a pet. I've tuned in to it to work out if a physical symptom is serious enough to warrant medical investigation or is simply a manifestation of stress.

I even once used this knowing to get off an aeroplane which didn't feel safe despite the noise around me that tried to convince me *I was wrong, I was tired, I was batshit crazy, I was being ridiculous, I was spoiling a long-awaited holiday, I was inconveniencing and delaying others, I was being selfish.*

As it turns out, all it takes is trust to let yourself know what you know.

Postscript: later that day, Zed and I got on another plane and made it to Tasmania for our honeymoon. The pendulum confirmed what I knew – it was safe to fly.

Joanne Fedler is the internationally bestselling author of ten books, including Your Story: how to write it so others will want to read it. *She is a writing mentor, entrepreneur, speaker and publisher of Joanne Fedler Media. Her transformational writing courses and Masterclasses teach people to take their lives and turn them into stories they can gift as narratives of wisdom to others.*

Self-esteem means knowing that you are the dream.

OPRAH

Knowing with Michelle Weitering

A Story of Knowing:
By Michelle Weitering – AKA Mickey Martin

I've always been blessed and lucky in life, despite all the difficulties. Even at a young age, I always believed everything would work out the way it was meant to – and whichever way that turned out to be, I knew I was going to be all right, and that anything great could happen, no matter what happened.

I was nothing special, yet I was entirely marvellous. I had the ability to be kind, even on the darkest of days. Even as a little girl, I felt that certainly had to be some kind of skill, for sure. My cup, no matter how thirsty the world was, was always half full and I was happy to share it with all.

My first two decades in this world were certainly no picnic, yet character-building. As one half of twin girls, I started my first couple of years in life watching my father abuse my mother; thankfully Mum did divorce him in the end. It was such a difficult thing for her to do, especially in the '70s when there was so much stigma attached to divorce; the shame and embarrassment for a woman to become a single parent was not accepted in that era. Mum's self-esteem took a beating, and as a result she ended up with another man who was just as delightful as the first, and so the cycle continued; we were all subjected to years of physical and emotional abuse at his hand. Mum worked full time, and my twin and I were ruled by our stepfather, who felt the need to inform us daily that we were stupid and useless, along with the buckle end of his belt. As each word cut through my growing soul, and each belting stung more than the time before, I knew, no matter how many times I was degraded and made to feel worthless, I was not.

I bravely bent over whilst he belted my sky-clad ass, knowing he had issues, and often wondered what they were as he administered each painful tear upon my flesh—but, as a kid, you don't think to raise such questions. I was just trying to survive, day in, day out, and cope with going to school and being a decent student (God I hated maths!), make a few friends, and get through the next day as best I could. And on those terrible days, you would find me hiding up the walnut tree with a book, waiting till Mum got home from work. Although the abuse would be inflicted for many years, I knew it couldn't last forever, and that one day, I'd be free. I knew that never again would I face such abuse; even through those tough, dark days I still knew everything would turn out okay. I don't know how I knew this; I guess I just felt it. Deep down inside me was a feeling, and it was a feeling of steady hope; it was these feelings that carried the younger me through the darkest days where I would have otherwise drowned in tears. Knowing that, and believing it, was my life raft. My Knowing was my saviour.

Unfortunately, like too many children, my twin and I were sexually abused when we were eleven by someone who was considered a close family friend at the time. This resulted in three moves in our first year of high school alone. Attending three high schools in a matter of eight months was no easy feat for a young teen, and this too would be another character-building process, along with social worker visits, police interviews and a court case hearing. I remember that day in court as clearly as though it were yesterday. Both my sister and I had to stand in the witness box and face our predator; if that were not daunting and nerve-wracking enough, my twin and I were absolutely mortified that Mum had dressed us in matching tartan skirts with Big Bird socks that came up to our knees! I mean, seriously: Big Bird does *not* go with tartan. To this day, I do not feel sorry for that skinny girl standing nervously in court while the prosecutor belittled her. I just remember her thinking, 'I can't believe Mum made us wear this!' My God. Kids are so resilient.

Bless my mother's heart—she was heartbroken and a nervous wreck herself that day and for the many days and years that followed. While trying to protect us she was constantly navigating through her own muddy waters of guilt that somehow, she hadn't done enough. When we were sixteen we went to our first Blue Light Disco dressed in ankle-length skirts and Daffy Duck wind cheaters. It was another mortifying moment we would never forget, even though no one else probably even noticed, let alone remembered. When I look back now through the eyes of that impressionable, young eleven-year-old girl, I am fascinated by what the mind holds onto and uses as methods of survival. And as horrific as that particular incident had been on our young lives, and the scars it would leave on us at the time and for years to come, I now also realise that if it had not occurred, I would not be where I am, or who I am, today.

I believe, wholeheartedly, that everything happens for a reason. Everything. The great things, the horrid things, and all the things in between. Throughout those years of abuse the only thing I had control over was my mindset. My knowing that everything was going to be okay was the one true thing I could hold onto; it was my guiding light. Fate had one direction for me, but Destiny was constantly calling my name; and I was listening.

"Fate is the life you lead if you never put yourself in the path of greatness.

That's the direction your life moves in without any effort on your part.

Destiny is your potential waiting to happen."

I loved the sound of that and kept this mantra close to my heart as I evolved. And I have worked so hard to evolve; to become that happy, confident me who had the ability to do great things. To truly believe in myself. Those who, like me, have suffered chronic childhood trauma in the form of physical and emotional abuse delivered by an authority figure spanning a period of many years, know this can be very difficult, if not impossible to overcome. But I didn't want other people's mistakes, choices or crimes to prevent me from living a life I felt *I truly deserved.* I have faced what happened to me in my childhood, accepted that it was just a chapter in my book, turned the next page and moved on. I wanted to be someone who could help people. I wanted to be that person to inspire others around me to do more, be more.

I was so very lucky to fall in love with the kindest of men, and during our twenty-six years together, Jade has supported me in every choice I make. Even some of the bad ones. My greatest joy was becoming a mother to two gorgeous boys. And having our beautiful boys led me on yet another journey. This journey would not have taken place the way it had if anxiety and depression disorder had not gripped both our boys and taken them on a journey of their own. When anxiety dragged my eldest son into an underworld, our world was ripped apart. I hadn't felt such darkness since my days as a child and it absolutely killed me to watch my innocent little boy suffer.

I knew so many parents around the world with children

who were also struggling with this depressive disorder, and I wanted to offer any support or insight that I could. It was then that I decided to share our story and wrote *Thirteen and Underwater*. It took me five years to write and re-write this book, and it was worth all the blood, sweat and tears. I poured all my words, heartache and fears into something that I could wrap around another's heart, if only to help comfort and console them, too.

Having published my first book in 2014, a dark romance, I was so disappointed with the publisher, and knew I could only trust someone exceptional with *Thirteen and Underwater*.

It had to fall into the hands of someone who was passionate, excited and dedicated to the author's journey and the book's success. It had to go to someone who believed in magic, and who knew that by creating that magic, anything could happen. I'd been researching Australian publishers for years when I came across Karen McDermott and Serenity Press, and thought, 'Wow!' lucky authors.' I was finishing my second draft of *Thirteen* when sadly, tragically, my gorgeous mother passed away.

That day I lost my greatest love, my everything. And everything was put on hold.

But, as they say, timing is everything; so when *Thirteen* was set to fly, I again sought Karen McDermott and found her Everything Publishing Academy. What an absolute goldmine I had hit upon, where authors are assisted through every aspect from editing to publication. More research led me to Making Magic Happen Press. Well, isn't it funny that Mum always claimed I was 'off with the fairies', so to speak; so the publishing name alone had me at the get go. I sent an email and within a week I was having Face Time with Karen.

I remember being a mixture of nervous excitement. It was surreal; I had goosebumps on a thirty-two-degree day in Melbourne. It was the moment I'd been waiting for; she was a great woman and publisher I had been admiring for years and she listened enthusiastically to my story about *Thirteen*. Her big, warm bright smile, and her enthusiasm on the direction *Thirteen* could take was infectious, and once again I was enveloped with the power of Knowing. I knew in an instant that Karen would play a big part in my writing future and I signed with MMH Press.

There's just that thing about knowing, you know? And the day I finally met Karen was the day I did my first author talk at the Docklands library in Melbourne. And, once again, I knew. Karen has a soul, and an intuition; she is a person who goes above and beyond to help others realise their potential and live their dreams, if only one is brave enough to chase them. At my first speaking event, I was terrified — I suffer from, and have a serious case of, *glossophobia*, or fear of public speaking. Yet, upon meeting Karen my fears were allayed; it was this sense of knowing that I could overcome it, and with Karen's help I was able to put my fears aside. Since then, I have had to speak at numerous events and businesses in and around Melbourne as well as at the historic Crom Castle in Ireland. All this while *Thirteen* went on her journey around the world to the London Book Fair, was pitched at the Melbourne International Film Festival and was featured in several magazines, including *Ymag*. I was nominated for the AusMumpreneur Awards and was a finalist in the Regional Business Excellence Award. I have worked closely with mental health networks both here and in Ireland and have become an International author and speaker, and I have now signed on as an Author Shareholder with MMH Press. I can't begin to describe the pride I feel, being part of the team with such a successful publishing press. I'm about to attend my first Australian Romance Readers festival, ARRA, and *Thirteen and Underwater* is going into our Aussie Golden Logie Nominees gift bags for 2020 and I can't wait to see what happens next!

I cannot deny that this last year has been the most magical whirlwind journey, and all of these things just kept happening, all because I followed my instinct without fear, all because I knew what I had to do, and in the end I just did it. And my journey has been made all the sweeter with my husband, my sons, the best of friends, and my twin by my side, and a publisher who became my friend. And my beautiful, all-knowing mother, I know, is leading the way. Life has certainly been far from perfect, and at times it has not been easy; but the song of a bird, the scent of a flower, the laughter of loved ones all centre me in my Knowing. Knowing who I am and where I am going and who I want to be.

So, when I look back on my life now through the lens of 'Knowing', how did I know that life would lead me to where it has, exactly to where that eleven-year-old girl once knew that everything would be okay? Through the incredible twists and turns my life has taken, through the journeys that have unfolded, what I know is this: Knowing has led the way. *To know is to know.* I still know that Big Bird does not go with tartan, and I am thankful to have the greatest fashion sense because of it. It is such a long way from that little girl who climbed up the walnut tree to hide and read a book, but that's okay. And let me tell you something else I know: the view from here is breathtaking.

Follow your instincts,
that's where true wisdom manifests itself.

OPRAH

Knowing with Karen Weaver

In 2008, against all rational thinking, I packed up our little family, locked the door on a brand-new house and boarded the plane to Australia. I was thirty-five weeks pregnant at the time and we knew no one on the other side. We had five days booked in a motel and $13000 to set up a new life for our family. Looking back now, ten years later, I can see how it might have been perceived as reckless by outsiders, but this was an inside job and I Knew with all of my heart that what I was doing was exactly what I was supposed to be doing at that moment in my life. In my perception we are living recklessly if we are not living! I was certainly living. How are we to find our true path? How are we to live to our full potential if we stay safely behind the tight boundaries set by society?

It was terribly sad saying goodbye to my family, it sunk right to the pit of my stomach. When we arrived, it took time to find our way and a new home for us. Things were different but we worked it out. When my baby was born I felt inspired to write. I wrote children's books, which led me on to other things. I went with the flow of my Knowing, I trusted it completely. I did lots of self-discovery too. I worked through lots and, even though I didn't have any belief in myself as a writer, I started writing small pieces that seemed to resonate with people so I kept writing. I found myself as the Organic writer of a website and my articles were being found, picked up and repurposed.

My writing started to be embraced which in turn gifted me the belief in myself. That belief and courage is what led me to writing my first novel in thirty days. Again, it could have been perceived as a totally irrational thing to do given I had just given birth to my fourth child. But I had a strong Knowing so I set the intention and knew that if it was supposed to be it would flow, and it did. After thirty days I had a fifty thousand word novel. This action led me to becoming published and then in turn to find my true calling which was to build Serenity Press and the Making Magic Happen Academy.

I could never have known the journey beforehand, I had to trust that magic was going to happen and it did. I have been on the most magnificent journey since, all channelled through my Power of Knowing. I urge anyone who wants to live to their highest potential to reconnect to their natural ability to Know and you will be able to make decisions aligned with your highest potential and true purpose.

When time and circumstance align, magic happens.

Your job is to make the time, create the circumstance and have the courage to embrace the magic, as it sits just outside your comfort zone. The magic happens in the action that follows.

Know the rules well so you can break them efficiently.

DALAI LAMA

Knowing with Bernadette O'Connor

'How do you know?' is a question I am so frequently asked since developing my knowing to a level where I am able to access information that is not consciously known.

'I don't know, I just do,' is my standard response because I feel completely incapable of explaining the metaphysics behind being able to bring through information that is not known to the conscious mind. The mystery of knowing comes from the unknown and the power of knowing only comes with trusting in the unknown.

In 2012 I began my studies in Kinesiology, a natural healing modality that works with the body to restore balance to the energy pathways that lie within and around the physical body. When the energy of the physical body is balanced, it does what it is innately designed to do, which is to heal itself. Balanced energy in the physical, mental, emotional and spiritual aspects of a person enables them to be who they desire to be, feel how they desire to feel and achieve what they are here to achieve; in other words, to live their truth.

Prior to opening to my intuitive senses, I was a left-brained, highly intellectual perfectionist who needed to know the how and why of everything, in a desire to understand and therefore be able to control my world. With an undergraduate degree in science, I needed to understand the scientific basis of everything I was being taught in my kinesiology course, and neurology, physiology and metaphysics can explain how kinesiology works. Yet what I learnt a few months into my studies was there were certain things that the science couldn't explain because researchers haven't yet delved deeply enough into the metaphysical world to understand the vastness of the universe and the power of universal energy.

Working with others I quickly began being able to access information that was unknown on a conscious level, without even using my standard kinesiology techniques. As I immersed myself in my studies, I cleared blocks in my energy body and in evolving, I found myself opened to pathways of information that I didn't understand and my knowing or intuitive abilities developed exponentially. I found myself knowing information about others that there was no way I could know and the science couldn't explain my knowing of the unknown.

And so began my dance between the visible and invisible and fortunately something within allowed me to surrender my need to know how I was able to receive this information. I learnt to let go and trust in the unknown, which I now understand was imperative to my intuitive gifts developing to the level that they have. I cannot explain how I know the unknown, but I implicitly trust in my knowing and that has allowed me to live my life for the past seven years in a unique way, one that trusts in the power of knowing.

Knowing does not come from the conscious mind, it cannot be thought, it is a feeling that comes from somewhere within. To *know* is to feel and knowing is only able to be accessed with listening deeply to the feelings elicited through the experiences of life, and innately trusting in those feelings as an inner navigation system. To be knowing or intuitive is not a gift exclusively for 'highly evolved spiritual' people as many would believe. Knowing is a sense as present as any of the other five senses, yet this sixth sense is underdeveloped and underutilised by most people who have evolved out of *feeling* into their experiences and have been programmed to *think* their way through life.

The purest expression of knowing is a newborn baby and in observing how they experience life, it is evident that the underdeveloped intellectual brain is their greatest asset because they do not think 'what do I need or what should I do next?' Instead they feel into each moment and respond accordingly. If they feel hunger they will cry with a specific tone, and if they feel wet they will cry in a different way, and again in feeling scared they will communicate their fear with cries or screams. While an untrained ear will just hear a baby crying, those who choose to listen astutely will hear the difference in the cry and will feel what the baby is attempting to communicate about their needs, based on how they feel not what they think. Beautifully, babies do not think 'Why am I feeling this?' or 'It's not okay for me to feel this so I better ignore it and think something else'. Instead they innately listen and respond to how they feel in an experience. Unfortunately many new mothers struggle with the challenge of understanding the needs of their baby because they are meeting the needs of their baby from their head. They are not listening and trusting their innate maternal knowing but are instead trying to understand their baby's needs based on what they have read in books or heard from others. When mothers suppress the knowing of the maternal instinct, in their desire to 'get it right' they often walk a path of struggle, frustration and exhaustion. In throwing away the books, not listening to what others say and listening to the inner wise voice that is in tune with the baby, mothers free themselves to follow their knowing and move in harmony with their baby. This is just one example, where the evolved human brain and the intellect that is revered in modern society suffocates the innate knowing that exists within all people.

As a child, I had a strong sense of knowing, being able to read people and the world around me by trusting in the instinctive sense of what I felt when I was with someone or entered a space. I could not articulate how I knew certain things about people or places, I just knew; but in a world that values facts and reason, my knowing was often dismissed, and in turn I learnt to ignore it. Like so many children I evolved out of my natural state of listening and trusting in my instinctual feelings and began to think my way through life, in turn losing connection to my inner wisdom and that powerful guiding force.

The intellectual mind cannot understand knowing because science cannot map nor define it. It is an invisible force that accesses what is unknown and it is this power that was once revered — the wise woman, the shaman, the mystic, who held powerful positions in their world — that became a threat to those who could not understand or control this mysterious and inexplicable knowing. The fear of the unknown and the need to control it by those with an overdeveloped intellectual brain saw the knowing ones forced into silence, fearful of expressing their true self in the world.

If it cannot be explained it cannot be real and if it cannot be seen or heard it cannot exist.

These were the unspoken messages I received from the world and in failing to nurture my intuition as a child, my intellectual mind was able to develop and the more it was celebrated the more I valued it. My intellect equated with recognition, approval and acceptance and as I moved through later childhood into my teens and twenties, the more I strived to expand my intellectual mind, seeking further validation and at the same time suppressing the deep knowing that now lay dormant within me.

And while I recognise my studies in kinesiology as being instrumental in unlocking my knowing and harnessing my intuitive gifts, I accept that this innate sense has always existed in me and been at play to varying degrees throughout my life. Interestingly, I began studying kinesiology without really knowing what it was. Instead I followed a very strong *feeling* that I was to study this natural therapy modality at a particular college. I sought to rationalise the powerful draw I had to the course that I had seemingly stumbled across, yet it wasn't a rational decision that saw my life completely change. It came from a knowing that I *had* to do *that* course and as soon as I sat in the classroom the following week, I felt something shift in me and a sense of peace and contentment unlike anything I had experienced before. In that moment I was assured that I was exactly where I was supposed to be for the first time in a very long time.

In my treatment room when working with clients, I have always trusted myself and the information a client's body reveals via muscle testing, the technique used in kinesiology to access subconscious information. And I love being able to reconnect people to the profound wisdom that lies within their body and encourage them to become increasingly aware of how their body feels when they are in different experiences. Our body knows and is always talking to us through feelings, and when we begin to listen and trust in these feelings we are able to utilise the power of knowing to guide us through life.

The more I lived an intuitively guided life, the more I realised I had always had quite a strong connection to my knowing. The feeling of making choices from within rather than from the head was familiar, but as my intellect had developed and the noise of life got louder it had been suppressed. Once I began working with energy, I once again tuned into the frequency of my knowing to help me make decisions; the seemingly insignificant ones like where to have my morning coffee to the important ones like buying our home, connecting with my editor and publisher and embarking on particular adventures. Where I have my morning coffee may seem insignificant and some days it is, but on other days I get a feeling that I need to go somewhere specific. When I feel into it and get a niggle about where to go, I am often rewarded with little pieces of magic. The serendipitous meeting with the very person who has been dancing around my thoughts for the morning, the person who really needed to have that chat with me, or the person who tells me something and I get an 'a-ha' moment knowing that a piece of my puzzle has landed and I recognise the need to explore a particular path or opportunity. It is my knowing that takes me to that café or event or gym session or party to have that conversation or make that connection, and sometimes those chance meetings completely change the direction of my life or the lives of the people I 'accidentally' meet.

Why am I currently sitting in this café writing about the power of knowing? I don't know but I was certain this morning that I was meant to come here. Will I meet someone and have a profound life-changing conversation or will the silence and space that surrounds me provide exactly the right stimulus for me to write today? Again, I respond with 'I don't know', but I trust and sometimes I don't ever get the answer as to why I was guided down a particular path. I have become increasingly accepting of the mysteries of life and surrendering to the unknown.

My most profound life choices have come from my knowing, not from my head and I am forever grateful for whatever forces within me or outside of me nudged me hard enough at certain times to take notice. Eighteen years ago, almost to the day, I was driving behind my sister Brigid and our friend Luke when a 'hit' of knowing changed my life forever. Brigid and I had decided on the spur of the moment to go and watch Luke compete in a triathlon. While Brigid had gone to university with Luke and we had all become great friends over those years, I had not seen him for a couple of years in those post-university days. There had always been this *thing* between Luke and me, a feeling between us that we were both aware of on some level. Yet somehow we both knew not to act on it and as a result we had known each other for seven years and never been more than friends. Driving to lunch after the triathlon, Brigid in the car with Luke while I followed behind, I stopped at a set of traffic lights and was struck with the most profound knowing I have ever experienced.

I murmured the words 'Ohh…Luke and I.' It was so obvious in that moment that we were meant to be together, that I almost laughed that it had taken me seven years to see it. Or rather it had taken that long for us both to be 'ready' for this relationship. I did not doubt from that moment that he was the man I was to share this life with, and three weeks later we were together. Eighteen years on, neither of us has ever questioned our union. It just is and we know it was always meant to be, landing exactly when the time was right. As a wise woman so often reminds me, 'When time and circumstance align, magic happens'. On that day all those years ago, the planets aligned to bring Luke and me together, and who are we to ever question that divine intervention?

Love is you. Love is me.
Love is knowing we can be.

JOHN LENNON

In 2016 after working with a client, Tammy Guest, a naturopath who ran retreats in Bali focusing on adrenal fatigue, I knew that whenever she ran her next retreat I was to attend. While I was on a seven-week overseas holiday with my family, Tammy announced the dates for her retreat and it was only going to be three months after I returned from this holiday. My fears told me I could not go because it would be indulgent to go on another holiday so soon, that other people would judge me for leaving my children, that I didn't need to go on a retreat about adrenal fatigue because I had already healed my own and also helped others overcome their adrenal issues. And fear made some very valid points, because there was no rational reason for me to go on the retreat, but I kept coming back to the *knowing* that had clearly told me I was to attend Tammy's next retreat.

I trusted my knowing and went to Bali without consciously knowing why. And to this day, I'm not sure the exact reason I was meant to be there. Was it the connections I made, the healing I did, the writing that flowed from me or could it simply have been that one conversation I had with Tammy about my almost finished first novel? We spoke of my knowing that the story of Halia in *Let's Go Home* had been gifted to me to share with the world, and I felt a responsibility to make that happen, without having clarity about the way forward. It was then Tammy mentioned Natasha Gilmour, an editor whom she felt would resonate with my work. A few weeks later on meeting Natasha, it was clear that she was the woman to help me evolve Halia's story to the next level. Many months later, it was Natasha who mentioned Karen McDermott, a publisher who makes magic happen and navigates life from a place of knowing. Again, one conversation with Karen and I knew we had connected for a reason, for she was to be part of the team that was to share my books with the world.

Did I have to go to Bali to have that conversation with Tammy, for those connections with Natasha and Karen to be made? Maybe or maybe not, but it happened that way and if I was to go to Bali for no other reason than to have that conversation then it was worth it because my life is profoundly different, in the most extraordinary fulfilling ways because of it.

A couple of months after launching my second novel, *Beneath The Veil*, Karen spoke to me about a writers retreat she was hosting at Crom Castle in Ireland in October 2019. She suggested I sit with it and feel into whether I was meant to be part of the retreat and for a number of months I did just sit with it, because it was neither a definite yes nor a definite no. I trusted that there was more to be revealed and time would tell if I was meant to go to Ireland. Once again fear told me that I didn't need to go and stay in a castle on the other side of the world to write my next book so rationally there wasn't a clear reason to go, but I couldn't ignore the feeling that told me I was meant to go to Ireland. Whilst working with another energy practitioner to clear some blocks that were preventing me from getting clarity on where I was to take my business, it became very clear that I was to go to Ireland.

'Bernadette, is there a trip overseas that you are thinking about?' she asked as she tuned into my energy fields.

'Hmmm...' I apprehensively responded because I could sense that the next level of my purpose, what I describe as my *soul work* was to be revealed.

'Is there something in Europe? Ireland? I can see you teaching *Beneath the Veil* in Ireland. Are you meant to go to

Ireland and run workshops?'

I laughed nervously as this truth was brought to my conscious awareness. I realised I had subconsciously been hiding from this information about my next steps because of profound fear of transitioning into this space. There was a reason the writers' retreat had spoken to me, because it was the carrot for me to go to Ireland and step into becoming the teacher, the leader, roles that I really had tried to avoid!

Let me explain. I had been gifted with the story of Clara that became *Beneath the Veil*. It landed in my consciousness and demanded to be written, and I allowed myself to tune into the story of Clara, to listen to her voice. I had written her story and then worked to have it published and launched in the space of a few months so the wisdom within the story could connect with readers throughout the world and create powerful change. I felt like I had done enough, yet now the niggling knowing I had been trying so hard to ignore was telling me that I was to take *Beneath the Veil* to Ireland, share Clara's story and teach the lessons within the book with Irish women. I contacted Karen McDermott that afternoon and told her I was coming to Ireland — I trusted it was where I was meant to go.

I write these words less than two weeks after returning from Ireland, where I attended the writers' retreat, promoted my books at three events and presented on six occasions. In the three weeks I was away, I connected with thousands of people, had hundreds of one-on-one conversations, shared stories and healings, and still I am not sure exactly why I had to be there. Yet I have no doubt that I was meant to be in the exact places and connect with the people I did because I carefully felt my way through the experience, listening and trusting in the knowing that guided me the whole time. And for that reason, I had the most unique and powerful experience over those three weeks.

From the time I began my journey to the airport to the time I walked through the arrivals gate into the arms of my little family, I felt assured, fearless, content and profoundly at peace. I did not miss my family nor did I feel guilty about leaving them or indulgent as I travelled alone through the ancient lands of Ireland. I knew I was meant to be there and because of that I was completely present in the whole experience, which saw me unapologetically flow with the Universal Energy that I know was holding and guiding me. And it was in that powerful space of being one with the Divine/Universe/God — whatever name you choose to use for the force of *all that is* — that I was blessed with hundreds of experiences where I thought: 'This moment! This is why I am here, and if I was to leave my three children and husband and travel to the other side of the world on a *whim* then this moment is worth it.'

In choosing to live my life from a place of knowing instead of listening to what my head tells me I 'should' do I sometimes walk a line that isn't comfortable for me nor for others. When you make choices that go against the grain and seem irrational or confronting to others, you must have a strong sense of self, inner confidence and an unwavering trust to walk the path you are guided to choose. It takes courage to step out of the box and live according to your truth and there will be those who judge and reject you for the choices you make because they do not understand them as they are contrary to how they live and view life. And that is okay because they just do not yet know the power of living from a place of knowing and how it allows magic to happen, abundance to flow and joy to permeate every day. I know I am on the right path even as I dance in the unknown of what comes next and I trust as I feel my way through each day, I will continue to be divinely guided by a force that is far wiser and more powerful than me. In turn I will flow with ease and grace through my life, sharing my gifts with the world.

You need to learn how to select your thoughts just the same way you select your clothes every day. This is a power you cultivate.

ELIZABETH GILBERT

Knowing with Jane Talbot

In August 2011, in my late 40s, I moved from Scotland to rural Northern Ireland with my son, who was just about to start secondary school. I moved to join my partner (now husband), who had recently inherited a farm.

I'd always been footloose and adventurous, moving from place to place and undertaking all sorts of projects: I travelled a lot, I ran up and down mountains, I ran across Scottish islands with a rucksack on my back, I managed my own business and I even did a stint as a retained firefighter — on call twenty-four hours a day, every day.

Deep down, I knew that being adventurous was my thing. Whenever an impulse arose, I followed it: I jumped on its back and rode it as far as I could, holding on like an old rodeo hand.

When my son and I moved to Northern Ireland things changed. He was on the verge of being a teenager. He had his own life and interests, and he had more academic commitments, too. I knew we'd have to stay in one place for him to complete his education, but being with a farmer also meant that I had to be prepared to stay in one place for the rest of my life! Not only was I pinned to one spot for the very first time, but I was also committed to supporting my son's developing interests, which meant a great deal of ferrying around. My adventurous life seemed to be evaporating.

I took on local community development projects to help me to put down roots, and I certainly learned a great deal from those projects. However, in spite of the chance to meet new people and to gain new experiences, my life felt as though it had shrunk – and it felt empty of the thing that made me feel most alive: adventure.

On 31 December 2013 I decided to undertake a year-long project in the hope of bringing adventure back into my life. On 1 January 2014 I started my *365 Days of Adventure* project, a quest to have an adventure every single day of 2014. This would be a quest to determine whether it would be possible to live an adventurous life through a series of micro-adventures, through adventures that would sometimes not even require me to leave my own home (and would still give me time to make a living and to parent my son as well as I could). This would be a quest to reconnect with my own, natural impulse for adventure, a quest to find a sustainable way of feeling fully alive and fully 'on purpose' without the grand scale of previous projects.

The first couple of months of adventuring showed a fairly random pattern of impulses. There was no adventure planning: every day I woke up and waited for an impulse to arrive, and it always came. Before each day ended, the adventure had been done, each experience video-blogged for those who were following my project and, of course, for myself. I was keen to see if I was headed in any kind of clear direction. Whilst the impulse was always a clear signal (when it came it always made me feel fully alive – energised, playful and focused), I couldn't see the relationship between the adventures at all.

I tried (and failed) to overcome my disgust for Brussels sprouts, I learned some magic tricks and phrases in one of the Inuit languages. I learned how to sing overtones, took a course in animal communication and wrote a tax return rap. I learned some Braille and British Sign Language. I learned how to play chess, I kept a gratitude journal and I played *The Prosperity Game* (a Law of Attraction game). I learned about black holes, worm holes, multiverse theories and Einstein's field equations.

I memorised the entire contents of the Periodic Table in sequence using the Memory Palace technique, I hosted my own 'TV series' on YouTube (interviewing a number of my talented friends from around the world) and I even wrote the first ten thousand words of a romantic novel, having read my very first Harlequin (Mills & Boon) novel.

I soon learned that romance was definitely not my thing: within the space of ten thousand words I had managed to kill off five men (the last in a spectacular mudslide in Pakistan) and there wasn't really much in the way of anything romantic in the text at all. There wasn't a single kiss. There wasn't even a single smouldering look. However, the romance adventure taught me some important things: I really enjoyed writing and I was really good at conjuring up spectacular deaths!

For the first time in the project I felt like I was on some kind of clear track, heading in a distinct direction. Of course, it took me by surprise when my next impulse for adventure had nothing to do with writing at all. I resisted the urge to override the impulse because I was convinced there was a part of me which was much wiser than my rational self – and I was convinced the impulses for adventure were coming from this wiser me.

Next came a tree identification adventure, and out of that adventure sprouted the game-changer for me: an adventure all about tree lore. Discovering that we had a lone hawthorn on our farm, and that faeries are associated with such trees in Ireland, meant only one thing: a faerie-hunting adventure. I watched a YouTube documentary about how to see faeries. I consulted a Scottish shaman and an expert in nature spirits, and when I knew everything there was to know about tracking these creatures down, I set out to see them.

I had learned that the best time to spot a faerie was at twilight, at the in-between times of day – either at dawn or at dusk. I had learned that I should leave gifts for the faeries (local whisky and cream) and that I should keep a respectful distance (and that there might be serious consequences if I didn't). My husband and I camped out in the back of our van, within sight of the faerie thorn. It was July, so evening twilight came around 10.30pm and morning twilight around 4.20am. Although conditions were perfect for faerie-spotting (the mist was rolling in across the fields, the sky was clear and an unusual hue of mauve, and all that could be heard was the hollow hoot of a long-eared owl), no magical creatures were spotted on either of my visits to the tree.

Happy that I'd given this adventure my best shot, I returned to the van after my early morning visit to the thorn and went back to sleep. As I slept I had a dream. The dream was a story, set in its entirety on our farm – and it was a faerie story to boot.

Although I didn't see the faeries (and my rational self didn't really believe there was much for seeing), it felt like they had seen me and left me something for my efforts in the form of a story. Keen not to waste the gift, I wrote that story down. It took me seven days to create the first draft and then a few more days of hard editing. When the story was complete it was sitting around the 8000-word mark and the next adventure signalled itself very clearly: get it published.

I spent time finding out about how to submit a manuscript and about how to find a publisher that might be a good fit for my kind of work. At the end of July I sent my story off to an Irish publisher and then thought nothing more about it. I never really expected the piece to be published, but I'd had fun writing it and finding out about the publishing world: that was enough for me.

From that point on, creativity seemed to be the clear theme of my adventures. I had a go at creating visual art. I spent a month writing haiku, and I even coordinated *The Big Renga*, a linked poetry project involving thirteen poets. Heading towards the end of the year of adventure, I wondered what 2015 might bring. I didn't have to wait long to find out.

At the end of October, I received an email from the Irish publisher. It said they loved my story and would like to see the rest of the collection. Of course, I hadn't really anticipated this email arriving and there was no 'rest of the collection'. They asked me to write another story and submit it by the end of November, and in that moment my adventure sequence for the back end of the year was laid out for me.

The next challenge was rustling up a story out of nowhere. I asked my husband to take me to the most magical place he knew in the hope it would whisper a story to me. My husband took me to a place called Murlough Bay, which looks over to the Mull of Kintyre, Scotland. As soon as I stood on the shoreline, I knew I'd be writing a story about merfolk, but I had no idea what the shape of the story might be. I spent a good few days consulting various sources of local folklore, finding a little-known piece of lore relating to some holy clay at Murlough Bay. So I had merfolk in mind and some holy clay, but no story. And so I did the obvious thing: I asked the faeries for help. I asked them to send me a story in its entirety as a matter of urgency. (Just for the record, I am quite sane and didn't think this strategy could possibly work. However, I was under considerable pressure and had no idea how I was going to magic up another story. In situations like this, anything is worth a go, especially if it's fun.)

That evening I went through to the living room after a long day's work. As soon as I sat down – as soon as my mind was at rest – a story came. I thanked the faeries out loud and set about writing it down. At the end of November I sent the story to the publisher and by early 2015 I had a publishing contract.

For the next six months I spent every spare minute I had writing. For every new story I asked my husband to take me to another of his favourite magical places, I researched local folklore and I asked for help from the faeries. By June 2015 I had finished my first collection of short stories, but I had more than a book in my hand to show for my efforts. By June 2015 I had got to know my local area inside out. By June 2015 I'd got to know the folkloric secrets held by my husband's favourite places and I'd developed an ever-deepening connection with the local landscape, heritage and people. Through the magic of adventure, through paying attention to – and respecting – my own impulses, I'd managed to access something I always thought would elude me: a concrete feeling of being at home and a deep and unshakeable feeling of belonging.

As I prepared for the book's launch in September 2015, I reflected on my journey to publication and how the *365 Days of Adventure* had been a life-changing project for me. My year of adventure had taught me that:

- Adventures don't need to be physical challenges. Creative and intellectual adventures can make you feel just as alive.
- Adventures don't have to take weeks or months to be rewarding: micro-adventures completed in minutes can still feed your soul. In fact, micro-adventures can be extremely nutrient-dense.

- If you pay attention to the feeling of being completely alive (and follow its calling), it will help you to live a meaningful, rich and satisfying life. You'll feel like you have a 'lucky compass' inside you.
- It can take a while to get in touch with your 'lucky compass'. By playing and experimenting (and even failing gloriously), you can learn how to find it and how to follow it.
- There's a part of you that's a lot wiser than your rational self. That part of you is worth paying attention to. I think that wiser self 'drives' the compass and helps you to navigate your way home. It knows your True North, I'm certain of it. By following this compass, I've literally found myself in a place I have never been before: at home (even though I'm an outsider). I've moved from place to place my whole life and ached to feel at home. Now I do and this feeling has brought me great contentment and a sense of stability that has allowed me to take on more ambitious adventures.

Given what my year of adventure, and the faeries, had gifted to me, I made the decision to keep following my lucky compass way after the launch of my book, *The Faerie Thorn and Other Stories*.

Since my first book was published, I've seen my work adapted for the stage and completed a number of theatre commissions. I've taken a seven-month intensive physical theatre training program, written and performed a touring stage show (including original stories and songs), and taken both classical and musical theatre singing lessons. I've written more stories, set up an organisation to promote female writers in Northern Ireland, and found rewarding friendships and fellow adventurers in my local CrossFit community.

I'd say that I'm still 'on my way home' and that there are still many new types of adventures to come. I'd also say that I'm learning to apply robust critical thinking when my compass shows me multiple opportunities all at the same time. I know I can't do everything at once, but when my compass does the whole 'this, this *and* this' thing, I know there are relationships between the options that link to something much bigger and much closer to 'home'.

Almost four years on from starting my year of adventure, I'm more aware of what drives me and of what's important to me. Even though I live in a very small country, I feel I have a huge amount of space to play in – and a huge amount of freedom to be who I really am. Not only do I feel more connected to myself, I feel more connected to others too. And, most of all, I feel excited at the prospect of what lies ahead – even though I have absolutely no idea what that might be. (Secretly, I really hope the tango features somewhere. Just putting it out there …)

Jane Talbot is an English writer, storyteller and theatre-maker based in Northern Ireland. You can find out more about her '365 Days of Adventure' project here: https://janetalbot.com/adventure-blog/ You can find out more about her writing and performance work here: www.janetalbotwriter.com

*Knowing things is magical,
if other people don't know them.*

TERRY PRATCHETT

Knowing with Elizabeth Gilbert

Dear Ones—

START KNOWING.

This is something I wrote in my journal a few months ago.

These words came to me through a powerful internal voice.

Allow me to explain.

I hear voices sometimes.

It's cool. Don't be alarmed. It's all good. I'm willing to bet you hear voices sometimes, too.

AT LEAST I HOPE YOU DO.

Every powerful woman I know is guided by voices.

Here's a story:

I have a brilliant friend who used to work in academia. She told me once that she'd been conducting a series of interviews of accomplished women, for a research project about women's success in the workplace. On the outside, all these women appeared to have nothing in common. They came from all different cultural and ethnic backgrounds, and all worked in different fields — corporate and non-profit, secular and religious. But each woman carried herself with confidence and ease, and all of them had become quite powerful in their own corners of the world. When my friend asked these women how they had gotten so far, they all began by dutifully reporting the same sorts of standard statements about the importance of hard work, and cultivating discipline, and fostering good professional contacts, and staying positive, and uplifting other women, and seeking out mentors, and blah, blah, blah…

Sounds perfectly logical, right?

But then there would come a moment in each interview where EVERY SINGLE ONE OF THESE WOMEN would seem to get bored with the questions, or maybe she was just feeling mischievous. Then each woman (EVERY SINGLE ONE OF THEM!) would ask my friend to turn off the recording device. Then the woman would lean in really close to my friend, and say in a conspiratorial whisper, 'But do you want to hear what REALLY happened?' And then EVERY SINGLE ONE OF THOSE WOMEN would report how — at some point in her life — she had heard a voice. A mystical voice. An otherworldly voice. A powerful and certain voice. A commanding voice. A voice that could not be explained away rationally. And each of these women reported that this voice had told her exactly what she needed to do next. And she had done it.

'I know it sounds crazy...' they would say. But it was true.

They had heard a voice, and they had followed the voice.

It hadn't been easy for any of them, they reported. The voices often told them to do really, really hard things — things that often felt like total disruptions of their lives.

Maybe the voice had said, 'It's time for you to move to Los Angeles now' — even though the woman had just signed a lease on an apartment in Houston.

Or maybe the voice had said, 'It's time for you to go to medical school' — even though she'd just had a baby.

Or maybe the voice had said, 'It's time for you to leave that boyfriend' — even though her parents really liked him.

Or maybe the voice had said, 'This religious path is no longer authentic or meaningful for you' — even though she had been raised by fundamentalists.

Or maybe the voice had said, 'It's time for you to learn

Mandarin' — even though she'd never been to China.

But the voice had come. And whatever the voice said, the woman in question had taken the enormous risk of deciding to follow it. Even when it was inconvenient. Even when it was challenging. Even when it seemed prohibitively expensive. Even when it meant cutting her losses and walking away from any sense of security whatsoever. Even when it cost her the approval of friends and family. Even when everyone thought she was insane.

And THAT'S how she had gotten there, to her place of power in the world. It really had nothing to do with professional contacts, or mentors...it was just that she heard a voice, and she chose to listen.

EVERY SINGLE ONE OF THEM.

So.

I hear voices, too.

I heard voices when I was a teenager, saying, 'You are meant to be a writer,' and when people said, 'But how will you make a living at THAT?', those voices were still like, 'Yeah, whatever... you are meant to be a writer.' And when I got rejection letters for years and years, and nobody was interested in my work, those voices were STILL like, 'Yup...you are definitely meant to be a writer.' And those voices STILL tell me I'm meant to be a writer. I'll stop writing when the voices stop telling me to write.

I heard voices telling me to move to New York City when I was young. I heard voices telling me that it was imperative that I see the world, and that I learn how to travel alone as a woman — no matter what the cost or risk. I heard voices telling me not to settle for the security of getting a 'real job' — but instead to just work odd jobs, and to keep traveling, and to keep writing, and to keep gambling everything for creativity and an exploratory life of the mind. (You guys, I can't tell you how many times the voices tell me never to choose security over creativity. It's exhausting and sometimes scary. But they seem to REALLY MEAN IT.)

When I was in my twenties, I heard voices warning me not to get married, but I went ahead and got married anyway (Side note: It's REALLY HARD for young women to push back against the forces of culture and tradition sometimes) and then I SERIOUSLY started hearing voices when I was thirty years old, and firmly married, and living in a shiny new house in the suburbs, and my mind and body were absolutely falling to pieces, and I was supposed to be trying to have a baby that year, and the voices started screaming, 'OH, NO YOU DON'T, MISSY!' And then I had to leave everything behind, in order to re-calibrate my path to my own truth. (This was awfully inconvenient and horrible and expensive and terrifying. And it's REALLY HARD to decide not to have a child in a culture that still tells women that having children, ultimately, is the only thing that shall fulfil them. But the voices were like 'NOPE', so I had to leave it all behind. We call that 'a course adjustment'. It's never easy. But you don't get to chart your own life without making some pretty hard core course corrections along the way.)

I still hear voices. I heard voices this spring telling me to leave everything behind yet again, and to gamble everything for love. (Very hard. Very scary. Very ACCURATE.)

Where do the voices come from? Beats me. You can call it 'intuition'. You can call it 'the still small voice within'. You can call it your 'inner compass'. You can call it 'God'. You can call it 'Angels'. You can call it your 'spirit guides'. You can call it your 'gut instinct'. You can call it your 'dead ancestors speaking though you'. You can call it 'the flow'...but whatever it is, those voices exist. And you must train yourself to trust them, and to risk everything in order to follow them.

Notice that I didn't say, 'You must train yourself to hear them.'

I don't think you have to practice hearing them. I think they are always talking to you. I just think you have to train yourself to TRUST THEM. That's the hard part.

Learning to trust those voices is a practice that you can cultivate. Just like any other craft or skill, it is worth the effort to learn how to master it.

So...Today, I want to tell you what my voices have started telling me lately.

It's just these two words:

START KNOWING.

Here's the thing about my voices. They can be merciless. They are not always sweet and gentle. Sure, there are times when my voices say, 'Poor baby! Poor little small one...we are so sorry that you are suffering, please take care of yourself, and lie down in a soft and safe place with a warm towel over your head'...but there are also times when my voices are like, 'Oh for God's sake, FIND YOUR STRENGTH. Grow a fucking spine, woman, and take the action you need to take right now, and stop wasting time...we didn't send you here to let you pretend to be damn weak.' (Interesting side note: The difference between THAT voice and my dark internal voice of self-hatred is that the dark internal voice of self-hatred says, 'You're such a baby, you aren't worthy, you are a scum person, just curl up on the floor in a pile of dirty towels and die,' but the mystical all-knowing voice says, 'We love you too much to let you keep pretending that you are so powerless...COME ON! Let's DO THIS! GROW A FUCKING SPINE! WE HAVE THINGS TO DO! WE HAVE A DESTINY TO CREATE! STAND UP OFF THE FLOOR!!!! LET'S GOOOOOOO!!!!!' See the difference? Good.)

There have been times in my life (this year, among them) where my voices have needed to get really firm with me. They have challenged me, and they have pushed back against my arguments. They will hold my face in the truth and make me look at it, even when the truth hurts. They will not baby me. They refuse to enable me. This is good. They will not say, 'It's OK, honey! Don't worry! It's all good! It doesn't matter — you're doing your best, and everyone's human!', but instead they say, 'Actually, honey, it's NOT ALL GOOD. This situation is NOT OK, and the way you are behaving is NOT GOOD ENOUGH FOR YOU, and it's time for you to grow a spine, and challenge yourself more, get creative, and change everything. Let's GO!'

But mostly, this year, my voices have been saying to me just these two words: 'START KNOWING.'

Anytime I am faced with a dilemma, and I start to feel very small and confused, and I hear myself saying, 'I don't know what to do!', some voice from deep within me rises in full power and says, 'START KNOWING.'

(I even wrote it down in my journal one day, for my entire entry that day. So that is what this picture is all about START KNOWING.)

What my voices are challenging me is to realise that when I am feeling sad and scared and small, and I keep saying, 'I don't know what to do!' — the truth is that usually I DO know. In fact, my voices are pretty certain that I always know.

*Being at ease with knowing is
crucial for answers to come.*

ECKHART TOLLE

Somewhere, deep within me, I have always known what I need to do. I just don't want to do it sometimes, because it's too hard, or too scary, or seems too wild or too risky. Or I don't want to hurt anyone. Or I don't want to be judged. Or I don't want to lose what I have already attained. But still — I do know. Secretly, I do know. And my voices get impatient with me, because they're like, 'Look, lady, we don't have forever, OK? You have all the information you need. Nothing will change now unless you change it. Make a move right here. Stop pretending you don't know what you need to do. START KNOWING.'

I'm sensing this in so many women whom I encounter these days, too. They seem stuck and frustrated and confused and insecure and afraid. They have grown too comfortable/uncomfortable in the realm of 'not knowing' what to do. They come up to me at my speaking events, and they introduce themselves by telling me about their injuries and their wounds. Before they have even told me what they want to create in this world, or who they long to become, they tell me the worst thing that has ever happened to them. Then I hear them start spinning and spinning and spinning the same story they've been telling for years about what happened to them, and how it damaged them, and what they want, but what they aren't getting, and why they can't change it, and why this situation is impossible, and what they wish would happen, and why can't it all be different, and why it's too late...and then they say, 'I just don't know what to do!'

And I swear to God, this fearsome strong voice starts to rise out from the centre of my spine, and all I want to do is take that woman by her shoulders, shake her, and shout at the top of my lungs: 'START KNOWING!'

(But in a loving way. I love you all! Seriously, I love you guys! Smiley face! You go, girl!)

But seriously...this voice that rises within me is not a voice of judgment or contempt. It's not a disgusted voice. This is just the voice of the Archangel of Womanhood — a divine force who cannot abide seeing any woman who has ANY power in her life pretending that she has no power in her life. Not you, not me, not your sisters, not your daughters, not your mothers. She just can't take it anymore. So voice of the Archangel of Womanhood says (out of a sense of fierce but merciless compassion, and a desire to liberate us all), 'START KNOWING!'

Yes, it's hard. Of course it's hard. What did you think — it would be easy? Did you think they would just hand your destiny to you, cost-free? Yes, you might have to risk everything. Yes, you might have to cut your losses. Yes, some people will hate it. Yes, some people may never understand and never forgive you. Yes, you may walk away from the situation with a permanent scar, or a bad limp, or a battered heart. Yes, yes, yes, blah, blah, blah...

But come ON!

START KNOWING.

Stop saying, 'I don't know what to do!' Because I believe that — somewhere deep in your centre — there is some powerful truth about your life which YOU ALREADY DO KNOW.

If you're afraid of making a hasty decision, just remember that the alternative is to stay stuck in the same bullshit garbage death swamp you've been stuck in for years. (I say that lovingly! I love you! Smiley face!)

So start knowing. Start knowing what you already know.

Knowing yourself is to be rooted in being, instead of lost in your mind.

ECKHART TOLLE

Start knowing what is so damn obvious about your life that a perfect stranger could see the problem, if you told her about your situation in a five-minute conversation. Start knowing that you will no longer degrade yourself with the illusion that you are powerless, that you're in a trap. (Here's the evidence of that: Tell me your story of how powerless you are, and I will find you a story of a woman who was in EXACTLY the same situation, and she changed it. I know...that sounds harsh. But it's true. Start knowing that it's true.)

Start knowing that you have far more agency than you think. Start knowing that the story you've been telling yourself about your limitations, or your helplessness in this situation, is NO LONGER GOOD ENOUGH FOR YOU. Start being honest with yourself about something that your body has been trying to tell you for years. (Listen to your body's pain — IT KNOWS. The body always knows. The body knows exactly the thing that is causing you suffering, and holding you back. I had a boyfriend once who I was madly in love with, but every time I got in his bed, my body would explode into pain, because my body already knew, 'This man is no good for you.' I didn't want to know it, because I was blinded by love — but my body knew. Start knowing what your body already knows.)

Start knowing the kind of woman you need to become — so that your daughters can have a better chance of becoming that kind of woman, too. Start knowing that the universe didn't send you here to this fearsome planet of change and danger so that you could practice being more afraid...but rather, the universe sent you here to this fearsome planet of change and danger so that you could practice being more BRAVE. (Stop waiting for the world to feel safe, before you live your life. The world never will feel safe. This planet has a nickname in the universe, you know. It's called: THE ADVANCED SCHOOL FOR UTMOST HUMAN BRAVERY. They do not call our planet: THE COMFY RESTING PLACE FOR PRACTICING EASE AND SECURITY.)

Start knowing how brave you are. Start knowing how resilient you are. Start knowing how resourceful you are. Start knowing that you are the descendent of thousands of years of survivors, and that have you inherited all their wiles. Start knowing that the Archangel of Womanhood loves you too much to let you keep acting meek and degraded. Start knowing how willing you are to walk away from all of it, if you must. Start knowing that there are no victims in this room. (I can't tell you how many times my voices say to me, 'THERE ARE NO VICTIMS IN THIS ROOM.' I hate it sometimes when they say that to me. But the Archangel of Womanhood is quite firm on the matter. There are no victims in this room, she says. Period.)

START KNOWING, you guys.

Try saying those two words to yourself in a very calm, very wise, very ancient, very adamant voice — the next time you panic. Just say it (START KNOWING) and then breathe. Then get quiet and see what comes up.

I promise you that your very next thought will be the truth.

It might not be easy, but it will be true.

And you are ready for it.

Seriously, you are.

Start right there. That's what every powerful woman I know has done.

Because the voices within you already know everything. But they can't work with you until you are willing to START KNOWING, too.

OK?
I love you. Smiley face. Let's do this.
ONWARD, LG

I discovered this post on March 2, 2020. Of course, Elizabeth Gilbert knows the essence of Knowing! It made my heart sing to find it and just as I followed my Knowing to find the post, I also requested permission to use it in this book because it fits perfectly with these other amazing stories. The amazing thing is, Elizabeth Gilbert wrote this post on November 28, 2016. I was writing Mindful Magic *at the time. I strongly recommend following this woman if you do not already.*

The moment when you connect with yourself and continue to connect with yourself. Knowing that you're right where you need to be and trusting yourself to take the right action to get where you're going. That is the core of Life Magic!

KP Weaver

IN CONCLUSION

Now you have an insight into Knowing. I truly hope that by reading this book you received some golden nuggets of wisdom to go forth and create a life filled with the essence of magic.

No matter where you are on your journey it is never too early or late to embrace the power of knowing. Connecting with divine energy in your lifetime is a true gift and something everyone should experience.

Remember to get to know the true essence of who you are and then you will have the ability to truly KNOW. There is no feeling quite like being confident in the path you are walking in life, for even though you might only see ten steps ahead, you have faith in your ability to make the choices that are true to you. That unwavering confidence cannot be measured in wealth as it ensures your priorities are always being met.

FEEL IT, THINK IT, ACTION IT.

Don't overthink the process, embrace the process. Make the effort to do it mindfully for twenty-one days and it will become more of a habit. Remember the Feel It part is the first and most significant step you need to feel right to your core. Give yourself permission to put yourself first. In doing so you will show up in the best version of yourself for others around you because you live through loving intention.

In Book 2 in this series I go into the power of loving intention and how by allowing yourself to embrace love, you will have a more significant experience of life and also the ability to fast track any opportunity.

We look at how intention is an important part of the process to achieving anything you hope to achieve. I strongly recommend you follow this book up with *The Miracle of Intention*. It is important to know the potential possibilities your intentions have and how to block out the busyness of life so you can focus on your journey and the gifts you have to give your external and internal world.

If after reading this book you would like to connect with me, I have a beautiful Facebook group for my readers called Life Magic with K P Weaver and we would love to welcome you to our community.

Happy Knowing!

First get to know who you are and then knowing becomes a part of your essence.

K P Weaver

Watch out for my next book in the series
The Miracle of Intent

WATCH OUT FOR OTHER BOOKS IN THE SERIES

THE *Alchemy* OF LIFE *Magic*
7 Master Gifts to Live Fearless and Purpose Driven
K P WEAVER

- THE MAGIC OF *Mindfulness* — K P WEAVER
- THE *Miracle* OF INTENT — K P WEAVER
- THE *Gift* IN GRATITUDE — K P WEAVER
- THE *Law* OF LOVE — K P WEAVER
- THE FREEDOM IN *Forgiveness* — K P WEAVER
- THE *Beauty* IN BELIEF — K P WEAVER

Lightning Source UK Ltd.
Milton Keynes UK
UKHW020837150121
377095UK00009B/198